The Mermaid in the Pond

Verena Kast

The Mermaid in the Pond

An Erotic Fairy Tale
for Adults

Translated by Vanessa Agnew

CONTINUUM • NEW YORK

1999

The Continuum Publishing Company
370 Lexington Avenue
New York, NY 10017

Copyright © Kreuz Verlag AG Zürich 1995
English translation Copyright © 1999
by The Continuum Publishing Company

This translation has been supported by a grant from
The Ann and Erlo van Waveren Foundation.

Printed in the United States of America

Library of Congress Cataloging-in-Publication Data

Kast, Verena, 1943–
  [Nixe im Teich. English.]
  The mermaid in the pond : an erotic fairy tale for adults /
Verena Kast ; translated by Vanessa Agnew.
    p.   cm.
  Includes bibliographical references.
  ISBN 0–8264–0926–1 (hardcover : alk. paper)
  1. Mythology—Psychological aspects. 2. Psychoanalysis and
folklore. 3. Jungian psychology. 4. Fairy tales—Psychological
aspects. 5. Symbolism in fairy tales. I. Agnew, Vanessa. II. Title.
BF175.5.M95K3813   1999
398'.354—dc20   96-8730
                                                                    CIP

Contents

Foreword

When adults read fairy tales, they are generally not only interested in what happens to the characters in the fairy tale, they also reflect on the meaning and the "moral of the story." With its fantastic images and dramatic events, every fairy tale conveys insights into the wonderful capacity of the human soul and of life in general to prevail despite difficult circumstances. Fairy tales show how we can find happiness, meaning, and wisdom: all we have to do in order to be happy is to take on certain problems and walk difficult roads. The possibilities for solving these problems can always be found by those who seek and who keep their eyes, ears, and hearts open. At first glance, it may not always be apparent how these wondrous stories foster happiness. Nonetheless, the series of interpretations presented here builds a bridge to greater understanding and awareness in your own life.

How? First of all, you should read the fairy tale. Make note of the effect that the story has on you. Ask yourself what thoughts, feelings and questions come to mind. By so doing, you will leave yourself open to the ideas that the author of the tale wants to convey. Even if you have never heard the story before, you will find that the fairy tale can become your own story. The story will become like one of those personal favorites you always think about, a story that perhaps unconsciously has served as a moral directive.

The Mermaid in the Pond will give you the courage to take a reading of your own "passion barometer." You will feel more capable of overcoming fears, more able to acknowledge what attracts you. You will be able to free yourself and, by trusting the wisdom within, lead a more intense and fulfilling life.

THEODOR SEIFERT

The Mermaid in the Pond

A Grimm Brothers' Fairy Tale

There was once a miller who lived contentedly with his wife. They had ample money and possessions, and year by year their prosperity grew. Yet misfortune comes with the night. Just as their wealth had grown, now year by year it began to dwindle. Finally, the miller could hardly even call the mill in which he lived his own. He was miserable. When he lay down to sleep after a full day's work, he could find no rest; instead, he tossed and turned in the bed at night.

One morning, he got up before the break of day and went outside, thinking maybe this might lift his spirits. As he was stepping over the weir of the mill, the first rays of the sun came over the horizon, and he heard something murmuring in the pond. He turned around and glimpsed a beautiful woman who slowly emerged from the water.

She had gathered up her long hair with her delicate hands and draped it over her shoulders so that it flowed down on either side of her body, covering her white skin. The miller saw that it was the nixie of the pond and he was so frightened that he did not know whether he should stay put or run away.

But the nixie let her gentle voice be heard. Calling him by name, she asked him why he was so sad. At first the miller was struck dumb, but when he heard her speaking kindly to him he took heart and told her his story. In the past he had had wealth and happiness. Now however, he was so poor that he did not know which way to turn. "Don't worry," answered the nixie, "I will make you rich- er and happier than you have ever been before. You must promise me only one thing: that you will give me the first newborn thing in your house." "What could that be other than a little puppy or kitten," thought the miller to himself, and he promised her just what she had requested. With this the nixie disappeared into the water again. Reassured and in good spirits again, the miller hurried back to his mill.

He had not yet arrived there when the servant girl rushed out the front door, calling to him that his wife had just given birth to a little baby boy. The miller was trans- fixed as though struck by lightening. In horror, he realized that the treacherous nixie had known that his wife was about to give birth and had tricked him. With a heavy heart he went to his wife's bedside and when she asked him why he was not delighted by the birth of his beautiful little son, he explained what had happened to him and what he had promised the nixie. "What good is wealth and happi- ness," he lamented, "if I am to lose my child? But what am I to do?" But neither his wife nor the relatives who had come with good wishes knew what to tell him.

In the meantime, however, good fortune returned to the house of the miller. Everything that he undertook was a success. It was as though crates and chests filled themselves of their own accord, and the money in the cupboard increased overnight. It was not long before the miller's wealth was greater than it ever had been before. Nonetheless, the miller could not take unmitigated pleasure in his good fortune. The promise that he had made the nixie gnawed at his heart. Whenever he went past the pond, he was afraid that she would appear and demand that he make good his promise. As a precaution, he never let the little boy go near the pond. "Watch out," he told his son. "If you touch the water, a hand will come out and grab you and drag you in." Yet year after year went by and the nixie never again appeared, and little by little the miller began to forget what had happened.

In time, the boy grew into a youth and was apprenticed to a hunter. When he had finished his apprenticeship and had learned to be a wily hunter, he was taken into service by the lord of the village. Now in the same village there was a beautiful and true young woman whom the hunter fancied. When the lord noticed this, he gave his young hunter a little house, and the two lovers were married. They lived peacefully and happily, and loved one another dearly.

One day the hunter was following a deer. When the animal leaped out of the forest and into a clearing, the hunter gave chase and finally killed his quarry with a single shot. He did not notice that he was near the very pond that his father had always warned him about, and after disemboweling the deer, he went down to the water to wash the bloodstains off his hands. But barely had he dipped his hands into the water, when the nixie leaped up laughing. She gathered him up in her wet arms and disappeared quickly beneath the surface, and the water rippled in circles above them.

In the evening, the hunter did not come home from his hunting, and his wife grew afraid. She went out looking for him, but since he had always told her that he had to be careful that the nixie did not get him and that he could not go anywhere near the pond, she soon guessed what had happened to him. She hurried to the water's edge and when she found his hunting pouch lying on the bank, she was no longer in doubt as to what had happened. Wringing her hands and crying out in grief, she called the name of her beloved, but in vain. She ran to the opposite side of the pond and called to him again. She hurled curses at the nixie but received no answer. The water's surface was as smooth as a mirror, and the face of the crescent moon looked up at her without so much as a blink.

The poor woman refused to leave the pond. With anxious steps and without pausing for a moment, she went round and round the pond. Sometimes she was silent, sometimes she let out a powerful scream, and then again gave a little whimper. Finally, her strength was at an end: she sank down onto the ground and fell into a deep sleep. Before long, she started to dream.

Fearfully she climbed up a hill strewn with huge boulders; thorns and brambles pricked her feet, the rain fell on her face, and the wind whipped her long hair. When she reached the top there was altogether another view to behold. The sky was blue, the air mild, and the grass undulated gently. In the midst of a green field bedecked with colorful wildflowers, there stood a little hut. She went up to the hut and opened the door. There sat an old woman with white hair who gave her a friendly wave. At that moment, the poor woman awoke. Daylight had long since broken, and she decided to follow the dream's bidding. With great effort she climbed up the hill, and everything was just as it had been in the dream. The old woman received her with open arms and offered her a chair to sit on. "You must have suffered a terrible misfortune," she said, "if you have taken it upon yourself to search out my lonely hut." Crying all the while, the woman told her what had happened. "Take heart, my dear," said the old woman. "I want to help you. You have in your hair a golden comb. Wait until the full moon rises, then go down to the pond. Seat yourself on the bank and comb your long black hair with the comb. When you are finished combing your hair, lay the comb down on the bank, and you will see what happens next."

The woman went home to wait, but the days until the full moon passed very slowly. At long last, the luminous disk appeared in the sky, and the woman went down to the pond. She sat herself down and combed her long black hair with the golden comb. When she was finished, she laid the comb down at the water's edge. It was not long before the depths began to stir. A wave appeared; it rolled up onto the bank and lapped up the comb. Before long, the comb sank to the bottom of the pond, and with this, the mirrorlike surface of the water parted, and the hunter's head appeared above the surface. He did not speak, but simply looked sadly at his wife. At the very same moment, a second wave rolled in and covered the man's head. Everything disappeared. The pond lay as peaceful and undisturbed as before. Only the face of the full moon glimmered on the surface.

Disconsolate, the woman returned home and, just as before, a dream came to her in which she saw the hut of the old woman. The next morning she again set off for the old woman's hut, and she told her of her sorrow. The old woman gave her a golden flute and said, "Wait until the full moon comes again, then take this flute and seat yourself on the bank of the pond. Play a pretty tune on the flute and, when you are finished, lay it on the sand. Then you will see what happens next."

The woman did what the old woman had bidden her. Barely had she placed the flute on the sandy bank, when the depths began to stir. A wave rolled in and lapped up the flute. Hereupon, the waters parted and there appeared not just the hunter's head but half his body too. He spread out his arms in longing, but a second wave rolled in, covered him in water, and carried him to the bottom of the pond.

"Oh, what is the good of being able to see my beloved if I am to keep losing him again?" asked the wretched woman. Her heart was filled with sorrow, and again the dream led her to the hut of the old woman. She set off again, and the wise old woman gave her a golden spinning wheel, comforted her, and said, "It is not complete yet. Wait until the full moon comes, then take the spinning wheel and seat yourself on the bank and spin the spool full of wool. When you are finished, put the spinning wheel near the water and you will see what happens next."

The woman did everything exactly as she had been told. As soon as the full moon appeared, she carried the

golden spinning wheel to the water's edge and spun busily until the flax was all gone and the spool was full of
thread. Barely had she placed the spinning wheel on the
bank, when something stirred in the depths more violently than ever before. A powerful wave rushed past and
carried away the spinning wheel. Hereupon, a fountain
of water jetted the body of the man high into the air.
Quickly he leapt onto the bank and caught his wife's
hand, and they fled.

They had barely gone any distance however, when the
entire pond rose with a terrible roar and flooded the entire
field. The fleeing couple saw their lives flash before their
eyes, and in fear, the wife called out to the old woman for
help. At that moment, they were transformed, she into a
toad and he into a frog. The flood that was lapping at their
feet could not drown them, but it tore them away from one
another and carried them far apart.

When the water had receded and both of them were on
dry ground again, they metamorphosed back into the form
of human beings. However, neither of them knew where
the other one was. They found themselves among
strangers who had never heard of their village. High
mountains and deep valleys lay between them. In order to
earn a living, they both had to tend sheep. For many years
they drove their herds up hill and down dale and were filled
with sadness and longing.

One day when the first signs of spring were just
appearing, both of them set out with their herds, and by a
stroke of chance, they encountered one another. On a far-
off mountainside, the man glimpsed another herd and set
off with his sheep in that direction. They met in the valley

but did not recognize one another. Nonetheless, they were happy not to be alone any more. From then on, they kept company, driving their herds together. Although they did not talk much, they nevertheless felt somehow comforted by one another's presence. One evening, when the full moon shone in the sky and the sheep were already asleep, the shepherd took a flute out of his bag and played a sad and beautiful tune. When he was done, he noticed that the woman was crying bitterly. "Why are you crying?" he asked her. "Oh," she sobbed, "the full moon was shining just like this the last time I played that song on my flute, and the body of my beloved emerged from the water." He looked at her closely, and it was as though the scales had dropped from his eyes. He recognized his darling wife. And when she looked at him and the moonlight shone on his face, she recognized him too. They embraced one another and kissed and lived happily ever after.[1]

Introduction

Many people grow to love the fairy tale "The Mermaid in the Pond" when they read it for a second time. This is exactly what happened to me. But why only upon a second reading? This story is not a "classic," the kind of fairy tale that one remembers from childhood. If one did in fact hear the story or read it, one probably repressed any memory of it. From a child's point of view, fairy tales involving mermaids (or *nixies*, as they are more accurately called) who snatch children do not exactly make for great reading. Also, the fact that the father in the story makes a mistake—and that his son has to spend his whole life paying for it with his own freedom—is something that makes the fairy tale unappealing to children. As everyone knows, however, fairy tales are not necessarily stories for children. Once upon a time, they were intended to be stories by adults and for adults, and this is exactly the case with this particular story.

For many years, I gave this story just a very cursory glance. It was only when I came to look for stories that focused on the issue of people overcoming fear that I remembered this particular one. Upon a closer look, I became fascinated by it. I have worked with the story in a couple of seminars and, over and over, have again come to the conclusion that it is a story full of hidden images. The more work I have done on it, the more questions are raised. If one allows oneself to be engaged by the story, it quickly becomes apparent how rich it is. It is composed of one subtle image after another, and by accessing these images we allow all kinds of feelings and thoughts to arise. Unlike some other fairy tales, this story does not elicit the feeling one gets when one encounters something that has been familiar for a long time. This has distinct advantages: one can deal with this story as though one had never heard it before. One can also give oneself over to images that are frightening without conjuring up all sorts of childhood fears. Instead, one can deal with the everyday fears that result from repressed attraction, and the depression that sometimes ensues. Reading the story also allows one to process the fears that one might have about separation, the feeling of being cut off from one's partner. It even facilitates the possibility of finding oneself again. By confronting the fears that this story elicits, one becomes aware of its tremendous depth. For me, "The Mermaid in the Pond" is an enormously rich fairy tale not only because of the wealth of existentially meaningful life situations it presents, but also because of the plethora of great images which serve the story. It sets up a kind of rhythm between two different modes, that of action and that of contemplation—between doing things and allowing oneself to grow.

The fairy tale gives us courage to seize life anew and, more particularly, to deal with one special aspect of life.

Misfortune Comes with the Night

There was once a miller who lived contentedly with his wife. They had ample money and possessions and, year by year, their prosperity grew. Yet misfortune comes with the night. Just as their wealth had grown, now year by year it began to dwindle. Finally, the miller could hardly even call the mill in which he lived his own. He was miserable. When he lay down to sleep after a full day's work, he could find no rest; instead, he tossed and turned in the bed at night.

One morning, he got up before the break of day and went outside, thinking maybe this might lift his spirits. As he was stepping over the weir of the mill, the first rays of the sun came over the horizon, and he heard something murmuring in the pond. He turned around and glimpsed a beautiful woman who slowly emerged from the water. She had gathered up her long hair with her delicate hands and *draped it over her shoulders so that it flowed down on either side of her body, covering her white skin. The miller saw that it was the nixie of the pond, and he was so frightened that he did not know whether he should stay put or run away.*

But the nixie let her gentle voice be heard. Calling him by name, she asked him why he was so sad. At first, the miller was struck dumb, but when he heard her speaking kindly to him, he took heart and told her his story. In the past, he had had wealth and happiness. Now however, he was so poor that he did not know which way to turn. "Don't worry," answered the nixie, "I will make you richer and happier than you have ever been before. You must promise me only one thing: that you will give me the first newborn thing in your house." "What could that be other than a little puppy or kitten," thought the miller to himself, and he promised her just what she had requested. With this the nixie disappeared into the water again. Reassured and in good spirits again, the miller hurried back to his mill.

He had not yet arrived there when the servant girl rushed out the front door, calling to him that his wife had just given birth to a little baby boy. The miller was transfixed as though struck by lightening. In horror, he realized that the treacherous nixie had known that his wife was about to give birth and had tricked him. With a heavy heart he went to his wife's bedside and when she asked him why he was not delighted by the birth of his beautiful little son, he explained what had happened to him and what he had promised the nixie. "What good is wealth and happiness," he lamented, "if I am to lose my child? But what am I to do?" But neither his wife nor the relatives who had come with good wishes knew what to tell him.

A miller leads a contented life with his wife, and their prosperity grows and grows. Things are going well for them; they are happy in a phase of life in which every-thing is flourishing. Clearly, they enjoy this state of affairs and, to some extent, probably take it for grant-ed. In all likelihood, they would say of themselves that life is treating them kindly.

As easily as prosperity came, however, so also does it vanish. Their wealth dwindles without any great to-do and without any apparent reason. As a result, there are demands placed on the miller other than just the capacity to enjoy good fortune. Yet, initially, he is unable to meet the challenge. He is now so poor that he does not know where to turn. It is possible that the scenario has to do exclusively with material poverty, which is difficult enough. Yet what arises are powerful existential fears. Unused to dealing with poverty, the miller is afraid of not having enough to survive, per-haps even of starving to death. Whether social fears are also part of the equation is not something that is dealt with in the story. We do not find out whether the miller feels ashamed of being unable to maintain his former standard of living and, as a result, suffers from feelings of inferiority. But it is also possible that this poverty reflects a kind of poverty in the relation-ship between the miller and his wife. After living through a phase in which they both took pleasure in one another, they now find themselves in a phase in which the relationship is not very sustaining. Although they are together, the relationship seems impoverished. Being poor can also mean having little emotional energy, feeling that life is empty and flat. For whatever reason, one feels as though one is shut out of the action.

The miller has a hard time dealing with this situation. He is consumed by anxiety. Instead of sleeping soundly, he tosses and turns as he worries about things. He also feels as though he should be doing something about the situation; he has to take responsibility for this state of affairs. In all likelihood, however, he is more preoccupied with the question of where to get more money from and less concerned with the issue of why he suddenly became so poor in the first place. He probably thinks about trying to restore the old state of affairs instead of reflecting on what this turn of events might mean for him and for his wife.

Completely consumed by fear, the miller loses sleep. By day, he is also plagued by worry. He gets up long before the break of day, leaves the house, hoping that he will feel better if he goes for a walk outside. The miller feels depressed in response to his changed circumstances, and his entire life revolves around the issue that is bothering him. He does, however, feel one tiny glimmer of hope: he thinks that by getting outside into the open air he might feel a little better.

Now a house is not simply a dwelling that protects us from the elements; it is also the realm of all that is familiar and all that we trust. In leaving the house, the miller demonstrates his willingness to experience something new, something that might possibly help him out of his predicament. He is empowered by a faint sense of hope. In keeping with his feeling of hope, the first rays of sun greet him crossing the weir of the mill. After a night of darkness, the sun rises— not immediately, but gradually. A first glimmer of light announces the arrival of the sun, letting him know that life will grow a little easier again. "Day" will in fact dawn again.

The events that happen to the miller in this story are things that happen to lots of people when they become depressed. Completely engulfed by their depression, they grow fearful that they will not be able to get a handle on life. They become plagued with worries about the future and have dark fantasies about what fate might dish up. They feel not only guilty, but also afraid that everything might take a turn for the worse. Yet in the midst of all this, there sometimes comes a respite. One morning, they suddenly feel slightly hopeful that there may in fact be a solution. From a symbolic point of view, people in this predicament also have to get out of the house. They have to get on their way if they are to experience something new. Being depressed implies that there is something crucial in life that needs to be integrated. It may even be something that is integral to who we are as a person, yet it is precisely this aspect of ourselves that we have tried to shut out. We have repressed and forgotten it. The function of depression may well be to compel us to deal with these aspects of ourselves that we have forgotten. Ultimately, life will become richer as a result and belong to us more. In a sense, we will "own" our own fate—something that can only be expressed by us as individuals. However, before we can achieve this happy state, we have to deal with all kinds of problems. Were this not the case—if the psychological issues and difficult aspects of life were visible and tangible—then we would hardly have felt the need to repress them.

Once the miller has decided to leave the house, the issues that he has been repressing immediately become apparent as soon as he has goes out into the light. Something stirs in the pond: almost synchronous with the first ray of sunlight, a beautiful woman emerges from the water. The story describes her long hair, her tender hands, her white body. The miller recognizes the beautiful woman as being the nixie from the pond—he grows afraid and is not sure whether he should run away or stay put. He has encountered the nixie, and the image of a nixie is conjured up in his soul. This elicits tremendous fear in him. Since the woman is described as beautiful, he may well feel some attraction as well. However, fear seems to be the dominant emotion.

Both fear and fascination are felt when something profound is animated in our psyche. We experience these emotions when we become aware of something new and when we sense that it has a meaning that transcends our own personal experience.

We know about nixies from reading fairy tales. We know that such things exist and that not everyone gets to see them. We know that when they do make themselves known, they bring with them a piece of fate: something inexorable is about to occur. The nixie belongs in the realm of fairy tales, not that of human beings. She is an in-between sort of creature, half-woman, half-goddess. What one sees is fantastic; it is wonderfully enticing and ultimately promises to usher in the beautiful. However, *ultimately* is the operative word here. Of course, there is also the element of fear. What does she want from you? Knowing all about nixies as people in fairy tales do, the miller also knows that nixies can be dangerous. Most surely, she wants something from him, but running away would mean running away from the very problem conjured up by the nixie. Staying put on the other hand means confronting the problem. To begin with, the nixie makes it easy for him. She approaches him in a very empathic way. She calls him by name and asks him why he is so sad. In calling him by name, she lets him know that she knows him, that she takes him seriously, and that now she also will take his dilemma seriously.

Being called by name—particularly in a situation in which one feels sad and insecure and like a failure—gives one the feeling that one is important. At a time when one is not feeling oneself, hearing one's name called is also something like the first ray of the sun. It reminds one of who one is. One also gets the feeling that, despite misfortune, one is still the same person one used to be. After an initial hesitancy, the nixie then entices the miller to talk about his concerns.

In other words, she knows what it takes to shake him out of his reluctancy to open up.

When we suffer from depression, it can be of tremendous help if we can manage to talk about what it is that is bothering us. For this process to be successful, it helps if we can talk as freely as possible. This way a light sometimes goes on, and we suddenly become aware of the factors that contributed to creating our depression. Naturally, a person with a gentle voice is most likely to be able to get us to talk about our worries, reminding us of all the people in our life who have ever spoken gently and with great tenderness to us. For the most part, the feelings that are elicited are reminiscent of the security of early childhood.

The miller tells the nixie his woes, and she promises to help him. In return for making him richer than ever before, he has to give her the first thing born to his household. It is a hasty solution, one that would hardly seem to cost the miller anything. After all, what could it be but a kitten or a puppy? As far as the miller is concerned, on the surface it would seem to be a good bargain. The miller reacts just like those people who seize the first idea that comes into their heads as a solution to the problems they are having. With these hasty solutions in hand, they feel reassured that everything has been resolved. They feel invigorated again and full of vim. At least, they feel this way for the moment.

However, the fear that the miller felt when confronted by the nixie should have told him something. But he is so happy to have been offered a solution to the problem that he does not give the matter any further thought. Nor does he seem to attach any real value to that which is "newborn," to whatever is new in his life. The death of the old makes him depressed and he would gladly be rid of that which is new. The nixie disappears into the water again and, comforted and in high spirits, he returns home.

The maid comes out of the house bearing some good news: his wife has given birth to a little baby boy. He feels as though he has been deceived by the nixie. In this situation, he ought to feel guilty—but what does he do? He blames the nixie, making her solely responsible. At this point, it really becomes clear that the relationship between the miller and his wife could not exactly be characterized as attentive. He has not even noticed that she is on the verge of giving birth! At the very least, it is not a loving, sympathetic, sharing relationship. How blind the miller must have been to his very pregnant wife! Is it perhaps the case that he does not want to know anything about birth, death, and change in life? Is he perhaps unable to accept his wife in the role of mother?

The nixie does not in fact want a puppy or a kitten; she wants the baby boy. She wants to play a central role in the future of the family. Henceforth, the son's life will be dictated by the promise that the father made. In other words, the father's problem has ultimately to be solved by the son. Even so, the problem is discussed within the family. In answer to his wife's question as to why he is not overjoyed by the birth of the child, the miller does tell her what has

SACRIFICING THE FUTURE • 29

happened. This is no small thing. There are in fact a
few comparable fairy tales in which the father or some
other person promises to give up the first newborn
thing in the house in order to quickly be rid of an
intolerable situation. In these instances, men not
only unwittingly sacrifice their own future and the
future of their children in order to attain a quick solution, but also generally keep what they have done
from their partners.[2]

The miller tells her what has happened. In all
likelihood, he would have been unable to keep the
secret to himself, since he is too dependent on the
help of others. Nonetheless, he states quite clearly
that happiness and wealth are of no use to him if it
means losing his child. He declares his love for his
child but by the same token says, "What am I to
do?"—a statement that demonstrates his underlying
depression. Clearly he is willing to accept advice, but
no one is able to make any suggestions. What does
not occur to him is to go back to the nixie in order to
strike up another deal. This is something he at least
could have tried. Were he able to do this, however, he
would not be the person he is. Instead, he seems to
sacrifice the future.

Sacrificing the Future—
A Depressive Way
of Behaving

Of course, nobody consciously sacrifices the future. On the contrary, we do everything we can to make the future secure and to ensure that we have a good future. We worry about all kinds of things. For starters, it is the openness of the future that bothers us. It could instead be a source of hope and expectation.[3] Of course, we never know exactly what the future is going to bring us. Even if we are aware that much of what will happen in the future is simply an extension of the present and past and the direct result of life as we have hitherto known it, there are always surprises. These "strokes of chance"—in other words, changes with which we have not reckoned—are what astound and surprise us. These can be both for better and worse. The open-endedness of the future means that nothing is written in stone. Even if something looks like a dead certainty, there is still the possibility that things might not go according to plan. This fact alone feeds the hope of a "better life." It allows us to fantasize about the future, to create utopias in the mind. Finally, it is the open-endedness of the future which precludes us from becoming too complacent and simply lapsing into habit. It is the quality that keeps us curious about what is still to come and about all the things that might become important to us. However, the basic uncertainty of the future is also responsible for eliciting fearful feelings. We act cautiously, functioning under the illusion that we might be able to control the future. We protect ourselves, we reassure ourselves, we emphasize things the way they are. We do all this in an effort to preclude change from taking place. In an effort to avoid feelings of profound discontent, we curtail our activities and bolster our lives so that the call of the future cannot be heard. By becoming enmeshed in the answers provided by the past and entangled in our own avoidance strategies, we sacrifice the possibilities that the future holds. We act in the hope that we will not make any mistakes in life. Fearfully, we hold on to what we have always had. And we hold on particularly tightly when life has already proved to be tough. We doubt ourselves and doubt our capacity to deal with difficult life situations. Nor are we sure we can cope with the life we have anticipated. In such situations, the open-endedness of the future is tainted with fear. We become fearful and melancholy, and, rather than seeing the bright side of things, we become preoccupied with doom and gloom. As a result, we become wary. In fact, we become so wary that it becomes impossible for anything new to enter our lives.

But no matter how we rail against it, the future always comes. If we have fortified ourselves against it then it comes as a rupture, a disruptive change, and an unwelcome interruption that calls into question our own conception of ourselves and the habitual orderliness of our lives. If we have an ambivalent attitude regarding the future, then it might seem tempting. With even fewer ambivalent feelings to encumber us, it might even seem enticing, even though we harbor some lingering uncertainties. This is the compromise that we strike between the hope of something better and our fear that life will take a turn for the worse. Compounding the negative side are the fears of disappointment and death, which is certain to strike us sometime in the future. The less fearful we are, however, the more the future fascinates us. We picture it in colorful terms and associate it with fantasy.[4] Obviously, our fantasies are shaped by our experiences in both past and present. But the less fearful we are, the more we can permit ourselves unusual fantasies. We become more able to indulge our longings and our desires, which are just an expression of the unconscious. Thus by fantasizing, we realize new experiences and aspects of life we hitherto have not known. Sacrificing the future, on the other hand, also implies sacrificing the fantasy of a better life. In so doing, we deny ourselves the option of getting to know our hidden longings and desires, giving them no chance to be realized.

In sacrificing the future, we attempt to keep everything as it is now. This is, of course, a futile undertaking since life just does not work that way. As a result, we feel increasingly threatened as we try and hang on to the things that seem to be slipping away. Yet even this kind of preoccupation is something we regard as forward-looking since it is a form of taking precautions, a measure that is supposed to make the future possible. Of course we cannot live without taking some precautions, but nonetheless we need to maintain a degree of flexibility so that there is still room for the unexpected. We even have to go so far as to expect the unexpected. We have to embrace the surprises, know that they never bring just good and accept that they also may bring bad.

Sacrificing the future, which is most clearly evident in a compulsive desire to hold on to the present, can take place in either the personal or the material realm. The bottom line, however, is that such an act involves sacrificing the self and sacrificing one's true personality. And this is one of the preconditions for becoming depressed. Because such sacrifice requires the capacity to change—to metamorphose and adapt—it is only when we succeed in embracing a policy of "dying in order to live" that we are able to see the open-endedness of the future. We become capable of living our own lives. To do so, however, means having a certain baseline trust in the process of life; it means risking that trust. The alternative is trying to control the future by holding on to the present. As in the example of the miller, this means rejecting everything that is new in life and saying that it is not worthwhile. Thus, people sometimes say that not much more can happen to them in life. In so saying, they diminish the significance of all that is potentially new. This is, of course, a sure way to preclude anything significant from happening ever again. They sacrifice the future, but at what price? They think that this will preserve the habitual, the peaceful, the immutable. What they get, however, is a fear-driven morbidity.

If we make such a concerted effort to guard against the future, then what we are in effect doing is sacrificing ourselves because we do not trust ourselves to deal adequately with the future. We are afraid that we will not be able to deal sensibly with whatever it is that life dishes up.

The Miller's Problem

But what is the miller's problem? In a similar fairy tale, the same plight befalls a fisherman.[5] Like the fisherman, the miller is used to living in prosperity and getting what he wants. He lives in a state of abundance. The stream by the mill propels the wheel of the mill which enables him to grind flour. He is in direct contact with the water, with the life force we so often ascribe to the unconscious. Furthermore, he works with grain, a foodstuff that is the preserve of agriculture and the goddesses of the fields. If one takes his life circumstances literally, then it becomes apparent that he could only become impoverished if there were no more grain or if the water ceased to flow. Either the harvest goddess is angry or he has to renew his attention to the river of life. Hitherto, life was like an abundant mother who gave her all for his well-being. Somewhat spoiled, he clearly never learned that there are not only times of prosperity, but also times of poverty. What he lacks is a certain autonomy and the creative fantasy to deal with his altered life circumstances. Like all those who are accustomed to receiving abundance, he does not cope with this time of poverty. He experiences it as an enormous burden and becomes depressed. For too long, a mother-complex has dominated his life. This was initially positive, but the downside of it is that now he is incapable of getting a grip and leading an autonomous life.[6] This also is apparent based on the fact that during the brief appearance he makes in the fairy tale, he is clearly looking for someone who might be able to help him. The help accorded him by the nixie is at the very least a double-edged sword. And there is no antidote to the nixie. One can conceive of the miller's poverty as a lack of energy, as a life circumstance in which everything seems empty. He has no source of inspiration and is engrossed by the fear of not being able to sustain himself. At the same time, the fairy tale tells us why it is that the miller feels so impoverished: the nixie in the pond has been excluded from life, and the feeling that the nixie embodies is what is missing.

The Nixie

Nixies belong to the realm of mermaids and nymphs. Also in this larger category are *Melusinen*. They are all considered creatures of nature who also have human qualities. They exert a particular force of attraction on human beings, and like sprites in general, they are in-between creatures.[7] As such, they belong to two realms, that of the water and that of the earth. Visually, this is expressed by the fact that the creatures sometimes have human torsos, while their lower bodies are in the form of a fish or a snake. Although they belong to the two realms, it can be assumed that when they leave the water, they try and take their place among the world of mortals.

It is also possible that this double existence denotes something about female nature, namely the capacity to maneuver in both the realm of conscious everyday life and the realm of the unconscious.

Alternatively, the story may allude to women's great proximity to nature, to animals and plants, for water lilies are also associated with nixies and sometimes represent them.[8] And if the nixie is so repressed that she has to use devious means to gain access to everyday life, then this would imply that the in-between quality of women has also been excluded and needs to be reintegrated into everyday life.

Nixies are regarded as nature goddesses who have lots of erotic and sexual adventures. Nymphs, the Greek version of nixies, were companions of Artemis, the Amazon moon goddess.[9] The picture of the many-breasted Artemis at Ephesus alludes to the fact that she nourishes all living things. When she is depicted as being a virgin, this means she is not defined in terms of any man and is not under any man's thumb. She is a great hunter who also kills what she produces. She is known as "goddess of the hunt, of archery, and at the same time, as the protector of wild animals, children and all that is weak."[10]

Marija Gimbutas[11] also sees Artemis as the goddess of childbirth, in the sense that it is she who opens the uterus and restores the woman to health after the birth of a child. Gimbutas sees in the Greek Artemis, the Roman Diana, and the Irish and Scottish Brigit, the successors to the prehistoric goddess of life and of birth. She was a goddess of the mountains, stones, water, forests, and animals—a veritable incarnation of the secret forces of nature. As the keeper of springs, fountains, and healing spas, she was the goddess of healing.[12] Regarded thus, healing can arise when something new comes into the world, when something new is born. In prehistoric times, the birth goddess also appeared as a bird goddess or as a deer.[13]

One could, in other words, interpret nixies as priestesses of the birth goddess. In popular mythology, ponds are associated with unborn children,[14] although the merman will on occasion fetch the children back again.[15] Belonging to the same constellation are fountains, which are thought to establish a link between this world and the next. As such, they constitute a kind of repository for the great existential experiences of birth and death. Supporting this idea is the image conveyed by popular mythology of three maidens conversing by a fountain.[16] These three maidens could easily be associated with the three *Norns* or the three *Moirai*, the goddesses of fate in Norse and Greek mythology repectively: one spins the thread of life, another determines fate, and the third cuts the life thread. Together they have an overview of fate. Gimbutas sees them as a personification of the old life-giving goddess.[17]

Finally, we come to the nixie, which is also part of this realm. To be sure, she has been somewhat maligned, and like most of the great female figures, her significance has diminished. For this reason alone, it seems sensible and worthwhile to salvage the figure of the nixie. The fascination and fear that she elicits give an indication that she is no ordinary woman.

Judging by the way they are depicted, nixies are invariably fantastically beautiful. Those who come into contact with people also seem to know just how to exert their powers of attraction. From the typical male point of view, they are also the greatest seductresses, creatures who lure men to the bottom of ponds and lakes. Insofar, they can be seen as a symbol of the kind of attraction that lures someone away from the everyday and, wherever possible, transforms him.

It is said of nixies that they have no souls and, for this reason, try to gain the love of a human being and thereby a soul. An alternative explanation is that they need the embrace of a young person so that they themselves can stay young and beautiful. However, their links with human beings are never permanent.[18] Ultimately, human beings always do something that makes the nixie either unwilling or unable to stay with them.

As to the consequences of mistreating a nixie, they are indicative of the nature of the creature: one can live with a nixie for a certain length of time, one can even have children with her, but she is not for keeps. The nixie is a transitionary entity. And this is something that has to be accepted, since that is just part of her nature.

The belief that nixies spirit away souls is based on the assumption that the nixie is a parasite that needs to feed off human beings. But is this really the case? Could it not be that it is just the reverse? It is quite conceivable that interacting with a sprite opens a person up to another dimension. For a brief time, one gains access to another world. We have to bear in mind that for the most part nixies are quite content to live alone, satisfied with their solitary existence and in harmony with the moving water. Is it perhaps just this capacity to live alone that enables them to be so seductive? The capacity to be in sync with another rhythm, that of the water? Finally, nixies tend to sit on the edges of springs and ponds. They sit where superfluity flows onto the ground. It is this too that accounts for their links with birth and death: they appear in places where things flow, where something is about to be born. And associated with their great beauty and strangeness comes a wellspring of powerful erotic and sexual feelings.

Nixies are intrinsically linked to the element water, the element that we associate with our emotional and spiritual states. Water is also the element that prompts us to dream. We use lots of water metaphors to describe our feelings and moods. When we are agitated for example, we think of ourselves as being "in rough water." We think of water "rippling happily," or an opaque situation suddenly becoming "clear like water." Sometimes we just simply feel like submerging our selves or resurfacing.

If one asks people these days about the sort of feelings elicited in them by nixies, their first response is that nixies are fairy-tale creatures. Thinking about nixies elicits fear, and this fear is staved off by banishing them to the realm of things that do not exist. A nixie is just a creature in a fairy tale. If one persists, however, and asks what nixies look like, how they appear in dreams and fantasies, and what fantasies are associated with them, then one is getting at something very personal. Secret fantasies arise that might be empowering: fantasies of erotic or even spiritual attraction. Someone might flirt with the idea of something "way out," and long for all kinds of erotic and sexual adventures. Feeling afraid of this, however, he will probably stress how dangerous nixies are.

The danger is seen from the point of view of the legend—the nixie can drag one under, make one lose one's footing. The fear is that one will lose one's head and do something foolish. However, if both men and women allow themselves to entertain their fantasies about nixies, then in some strange way they become more passionately alive.

It is a longing to get rid of all boundaries, a longing to come alive, and a longing for a counterreality that is far from the strictures of the everyday. Yet most people have the impression that this state must remain unattainable. They feel this way because they are locked into a kind of sexuality that has strict limits. It is only when they are made aware of this that people then start to talk about the way that their love relationships really are. Passion has to remain unattainable because it is either impossible in the existing relationship or because it is contingent upon the erotic-sexual terms of the relationship. Pursuing an attraction would mean that one risked loss or, at the very least, vulnerability. Instead, these feelings of attraction, forbidden love, and fantasy are projected onto women and, in particular, those women who are especially seductive, who seem different and who have something "strangely mysterious" about them ("tender and agile like aquatic plants, they ensnare you without you noticing"). It is, in other words, the indeterminacy of their souls that is enticing. This corresponds to our own indeterminacy, to the fluidity in our identity and the capacity to experience new things. This is, however, just what is so frightening. It makes us afraid of becoming entangled in something from which there is no escape. According to legend, this is the very fear that is associated with aquatic plants—that swimmers who become ensnared in their branches are unable to get free and drown as a result. This fear has little to do with water plants per se. It has more to do with a fear of nixies that has been projected onto aquatic plants. The water lily for example, the *Nymphaea alba*, is associated with nixies and is considered to be the nixies' flower.

For people of today, the nixie is an anima figure, a personification of the secret, repressed feminine in the psyche, behind which something very numinal and godly lurks. It is this which connects us to fantasy, which takes us out of the realm of the familiar and links us with our own true essence. Associated particularly with the nixie are fantasies of transgressing boundaries that involve the longing for eroticism and untrammeled sexuality. The nixie can be seen as an anima figure who has become locked into an originally positive mother-complex.[19] In this state, one cannot let go of what one once had. Once liberated from this state, however, the anima figure can contribute to a more independent sense of self. It is this attitude toward the nixie-like feminine and the concomitant attitude toward the mother-figure that must be changed. The naturally feminine must be integrated into life more fully, and the rhythms of nature, life–death–life, have to be respected as a normal part of life.

So, what is the miller's problem? To be sure, his relationship with his wife is described insofar as we learn that they have a child. The miller's wife also assumes that her husband will be happy about the birth of a son. What is missing, however, is an abundance of feelings that might transcend the prosaic, feelings that inspire both fascination and fear. Associated with this is the experience of love and death, of birth and death, of bonding and letting go— not as a punitive measure, because something went wrong, but because this is just one of life's rhythms. For too long, the miller ignores the nixie in the pond and, in so doing, succumbs to the languors of the everyday. Giving oneself over to habit may be comforting, but ultimately it leads to poverty. This is the state of affairs we witness in the fairy tale, an attitude that is antithetical to a sense of hope for the future, and one which always works against whatever is "young" in our lives.[20]

However, the fact that the nixie insists on claiming the first newborn thing in the house also means that there can be neither any sense of rejuvenation in the miller's life nor any real revitalization or hope for the future. Nothing can change until the problem is solved. Or put differently, once a longing for the realm of the nixie has been awakened in a person, then this problem has to be actively dealt with and processed at a psychological level. If it is suppressed even further, out of fear perhaps, then the feelings that are unleashed can become overwhelming. All new impulses in life can become focused on this one repressed issue.[21]

We know that the nixie appears and then disappears according to her own rhythm. For this reason, she is also seen as a symbol of eternal transformation. We should bare in mind that the miller expects his wealth to be present forever. He does not develop any kind of understanding of the cyclical changes in life because he does not want to accept change. He cannot accept the condition of poverty.

Ultimately, this fairy tale deals with the problem of how to integrate the realm of passion into everyday life. It deals with ways of incorporating powerful longings, and the erotic and sexual feelings that come and go, without the danger of losing one's identity. The fairy tale makes the point that life and death, holding on and letting go, all have their place. As a result, we can feel satisfied and happy when times are good. Furthermore, when things do not go well, we do not have to fall into a depression: we do not have to feel worried and apathetic and incapable of doing anything. The miller has to free himself from an originally positive mother-complex. Because he has not developed any further, he now experiences this mother-complex as too restrictive.[22]

The protagonists in a fairy tale are not, however, simply individuals, even though the problems they raise can easily be transposed to individual fates. Who now and again does not long for an untrammeled, passionate encounter that does not involve much forethought? Who does not sometimes wonder what if . . . ? For the most part, we are sensible and reject the adventures of the heart that could lead to upset, making us and others unhappy. Yet as a rule, our rejection also involves a degree of unavowed envy. In discussing this fairy tale in a seminar, one woman stated that one has to experience the nixie in a sort of controlled way, just enough so that nothing bad happens. However, a controlled nixie would be a captive one. One has to ask whether a nixie would put up with such a thing.

And which of us could assert that after a series of good days we are immediately reconciled to a few bad days, and without any ado, simply develop strategies for putting these to good use? Frequently when we are deprived of something "good," we react in a depressed fashion. And which of us can say that we are comfortable with the laws of nature governing birth and death? We may well want what is new or different, but this also disrupts our everyday lives—and the things that we want are precisely what we cling to so tightly. That is to say, we do want what is new—and if possible as many new things as we can get—but we want to keep all the old things as well. Sometimes we even like the appearance of change more than the actual thing. In other words, the fairy tale deals with problems that are common to us all. And the fairy story had the same function back when it was first transcribed.

The fairy tale also deals with common human problems in a different form. In the meantime, we know that the great goddess has been undervalued and underrepresented during the past two thousand years. The very nature of life today, cut off as it is from the rhythms of nature, exemplifies this point. We also know that many aspects of the great goddess live on in old fairy tales. Sometimes this takes a depreciated form in the figure of a witch, who for example hungers after life. At other times, it is the nixie who wants to steal what is newborn. In both instances, the fairy tale conveys the desire to incorporate these figures and to integrate the worldly wisdom of the great goddess into life.[23] From the point of view of this fairy tale, the nixie also wants to play a role in life and also has the right to coexist.

The miller's family provides a prime example of how to deal with these problems. It shows the way the nixie can be integrated into life.

Powerful Feelings That Are Longed for and Feared

Life is supposed to be lived to the fullest. If it is not, then we tend to try all possible means in order to intensify it. If needs be, we even try using drugs. When life is too "intense," however, then we try all possible means of dampening the intensity—by consciously exerting control, by employing avoidance techniques, by taking medication, and so on.

But what do we mean by the term *intensity*? That we feel alive, powerful, animated, elated—carried away by some inspiring idea. In other words, we experience intensity when we are seized by emotion. Experiencing intense fear is to experience intensity. So too is great enthusiasm in the experience of passion. In experiencing our feelings, we get a sense of ourselves, feel at one with ourselves. Our emotional core constitutes who we are as people. The capacity to experience emotions gives us the feeling of being alive; consciously experienced emotions are a fundamental part of our self-esteem and as such, constitute our self-worth. Yet, emotions also unleash a certain degree of fear. They have to be controlled otherwise we might be "overflooded"; we might only be able to react "emotionally"—and as we all know, this is a dirty word—at least that is what people think. Aside from this, we know that one can in fact repress emotions, and that then they determine our "rational" conversations and reflections. It would however be better to incorporate these feelings in such a way that they could be productive for human cohabitation.

These days, society idealizes people (specifically men) who are calm, cool, and collected. Associated with this ideal is a kind of longing for vitality, something that is often misunderstood as the desire for "action." The fear quotient is also on the increase and linked to this is people's level of frustration. This sense of frustration is often more or less repressed which results in the fact that people end up repressing their other emotions as well. Yet what people really need is to be less afraid of their feelings. They need to learn how to deal with them differently and how to deal with all the associated emotions.

The symbolic notion of the nixie brings up the issue of passion. And when passion is associated with the nixie, then it is clear that one cannot be talking about just a moderate degree of emotion. What we really mean is that we feel something very strongly. It is a feeling that is a bit unsettling, fascinatingly so. Every passionate encounter implies that we are completely preoccupied with the object of our affections. This might take the form of a thing that we are passionately interested in; it might be a person who elicits these feelings or an activity that has captivated our attention. It is not just that we are preoccupied: we are thoroughly monopolized. All our resources and our energy are devoted to this one particular thing. At the same time, however, we become invigorated as a result. Our life acquires added meaning and momentum. To be sure, whatever piques our interest like this not only makes us more interesting, it also makes life more interesting. Associated with this is an undeniable sense of great self-worth—at least, while the feelings last and we have the energy to entertain them. Life might be one-sided: we may neglect some things that we do not exactly mean to neglect, and lots of things that are an integral part of life might wind up getting overlooked. And yet by the same token, we do change as a result. We come to know aspects of ourselves that we had no inkling of before. The everyday loses significance, life becomes unsettled. At the same time, it is more intense, and our capacity for intensity is evoked. Should life become chaotic, then what ensues is a transition: we simply cannot stand still in the midst of great life changes and stay the same. The chaos we experience, however, ushers in the transition to a new kind of order. Like every other emotion, passion surprises us not only with its depth and urgency. We are also surprised by the direction our feelings take. We think that it is only when we wholeheartedly give ourselves over to our feelings that we have enough energy to take action.

And Everything Is Just the Way It Once Was

In the meantime, however, good fortune returned to the house of the miller. Everything that he undertook was a success. It was as though crates and chests filled themselves of their own accord, and the money in the cupboard increased overnight. It was not long before the miller's wealth was greater than it ever had been before. Nonetheless, the miller could not take unmitigated pleasure in his good fortune. The promise that he had made the nixie gnawed at his heart. Whenever he went past the pond, he was afraid that she would appear and demand that he make good his promise. As a precaution, he never let the little boy go near the pond. "Watch out," he told his son. "If you touch the water, a hand will come out and grab you and drag you in." Yet, year after year went by and the nixie never again appeared, and little by little, the miller began to forget what had happened.

In time, the boy grew into a youth and was appren-
ticed to a hunter. When he had finished his apprenticeship
and had learned to be a wily hunter, he was taken into ser-
vice by the lord of the village. Now in the same village
there was a beautiful and true young woman whom the
hunter fancied. When the lord noticed this, he gave his
young hunter a little house, and the two lovers were mar-
ried. They lived peacefully and loved one another dearly.

Good fortune returns to the house of the miller.
Here *good fortune* is defined as meaning that everything the miller undertakes is successful and pays
immediate returns. Everything is the way it was
before or perhaps even better. Yet all the while the
pond reminds the miller of his debt; it tortures him,
but since it does not exact its price, he is able to
calm his fears. In spite of this, the boy is told about
his problematic fate, and measures are taken to protect him. He is told to avoid going near the pond, or
else a hand will reach out and grab him. What is
conveyed here is the image of the nixie as a harbin-
ger of death. The fear of anything is, in other words,
very great.

The miller conducts his life just as before. The
terrible crisis is something that is now mercifully
behind him. He has just gotten a hint of the solution
of the problem, but its first manifestation is enough to
put him back on track. He can resume life as it was
before. He is content and everything functions well
again. He has emerged from the crisis almost
unchanged, and he leads his life as he has always led

it. He is happy and feels that he is doing pretty well. When he thinks about his son from time to time, he remembers the nixie—perhaps.

The miller resembles those people who, in going through a crisis, get a very clear picture of just what it is they have excluded from life, however, this knowledge is so invigorating and unsettling that they make no attempt to integrate this conscious awareness into their lives. They do not actively try to change things and depend too heavily on what is familiar. Like the miller, they too have guilty feelings on occasion—they well know that they owe life something—and like him, they occasionally think about the pond where something lies hidden and waiting to surface. But for such people, it seems to be enough that the problem has made itself known. "The son"—or some other person—is then delegated the job of solving the problem.

In the fairy story, however, the miller's problem can only be solved in conjunction with his son and the son's wife. Left to himself, the son would be helpless and at the mercy of the problem. In other words, both husband and wife must contribute to the solving of the problem.

One could see the miller's son and the son's wife as representatives of the next generation who must tackle the unsolved problems of their parents' generation. On the other hand, we could also see this as just the normal chain of progression from generation to generation. In every generation, there are certain problems that are repressed. This is the case in individual families and also in society as a whole. People are always subject to certain trends in society, which result in the fact that some attitudes and values are favored and others are collectively repressed. It is not immediately apparent that this is the case because if everyone, or almost everyone does something, then it just seems normal. Those who see that something is being repressed and comment on it are simply regarded as upsetting the peace. Thus, an entire generation can collectively repress certain problems. Because of the principle of the return of the repressed, these problems must then be dealt with by the next generation or the one after that. This generation will in turn repress other things that will have to be dealt with by successive generations. This is one way in which our fairy tale can be interpreted. Following this line of thinking, the female and male protagonists are regarded as models for a collective developmental process that is very necessary. From them, we can learn what ought to happen. Obviously one can also look at the story at a more personal level and see that a particular family did not deal with certain issues These issues become so pressing that in the following generation, they can no longer be repressed, but must be confronted.

If we want to avoid interpreting the fairy tale at an intragenerational level, then we could also regard the son as one aspect of the miller's personality. As such, the boy would represent a side of the miller that was "born" out of the experience of poverty and who is capable of solving the problem that is lurking behind his depression. I will, however, avoid using this kind of subject-level interpretation since the miller plays no role in the rest of the story. It also seems to me to be psychologically very apt that the children have to deal with the problems of their parents. Also significant is the fact that the developmental process of human beings is something that people are aware of, yet nonetheless do not really pursue. The force of habit is an enormous one.

In other words, I regard the fairy tale as an intragenerational one and, for this reason, now turn to the next generation.

Initially, the boy is told to avoid the great problem. The knowledge that if he strays into the proximity of nixie-like emotions he will completely succumb is something that has a potent effect. Initially he gives the said pond a wide berth. Apparently the nixie is not interested in the boy either; she waits until he is a man. The problem is not one that need concern him while he is still a young child; it will only become current when he is older. Nevertheless, from an early age he is prepared to solve the problem: he is apprenticed to a hunter. He learns how to deal with one aspect of nature and, in so doing, also keeps clear of the water.

He learns how to observe nature, the way it grows and changes. He becomes familiar with the habits of the animals, he learns to shoot and to kill. He learns how to channel his aggression in order to make a living. He stays in the realm of Artemis, the great hunter. Here he develops strategies and acquires knowledge and for the time being he is not yet threatened by the nixie. Using these conscious avoidance strategies, he is able to live well, but only for the moment.

What is depicted here as having something to do with the "nixie-complex"[24] can also be generalized to encompass all complex aspects of the psyche. This in fact is the case in all great conflicts that are very threatening and that cannot immediately be confronted. One must first recognize the problem and be able to delineate it. Only then can one postpone dealing with the problem until one has the ego strength to tackle it head on. This ego strength is something that one cultivates by developing aspects of oneself that lie close to the problem, but which do not actually concern the issue itself. The young man in the fairy tale, for example, learns to deal with the impenetrability of the forest. In the forest, there is also the possibility of getting lost and not being able to find one's way out—this too is one of the main themes of the fairy tale. In this context (albeit somewhat imprecisly articulated), one might also consider the notion of a person being overpowered by the unconscious. This would be similar to when the hunter is pulled into the pond by the nixie. Yet, there is a distinction to be made. When one cannot find one's way in the forest and is thoroughly and incontrovertibly lost, then there is still some possibility that one might be able to get oneself out of there. Standing on one's own two feet, one still might be able to do something about the situation.[25] The sense of powerlessness and helplessness is less profound than if one were to find oneself trapped under water in the arms of a nixie. One does not have to worry about nixies in a forest. Things are much more peaceful. By relating to nature, as does the hunter, one develops strategies for dealing with the problematic, even though the hunter does not tackle the main problem itself. In so doing, he develops qualities that protect his ego activity and convey a feeling of competence and self-worth. Aside from this, he works away at the margins of the problem, although not at the heart of the matter. With a more secure sense of self-worth, he can then go on to deal with really threatening problems.

The young man is very successful in employing these creative avoidance strategies. He is a cunning hunter and finds a woman he loves and who also loves him. They even settle down together, and everything seems just wonderful. Apparently they do not have any children, but he has a loving wife and a house— he has what there is to be had, and this would seem to be an expression of a successful life. At heart he is a happy man. He finds what he needs and has his house given to him—a bequest from his master, the lord of the village, who has replaced his real father. What he was not able to learn from his father—hunting itself, how to track an animal and keep it doggedly in one's sights, this active pursuit of life—he was able to learn from his surrogate father. What there was to be learned from his various father-figures has all been learned. But now that love is playing a role in his life, the problem of the nixie can reveal itself again.

Whereas in the case of the miller, everything stays the same and nothing changes, the miller has nonetheless raised his son in such a way to enable the son to solve the standing problem.

The Hour of the Nixie

One day the hunter was following a deer. When the animal leaped out of the forest and into a clearing, the hunter gave chase and finally killed his quarry with a single shot. He did not notice that he was near the very pond that his father had always warned him about, and after disemboweling the deer, he went down to the water to wash the bloodstains off his hands. But barely had he dipped his hands into the water, when the nixie leaped up laughing. She gathered him up in her wet arms and disappeared quickly beneath the surface, and the water rippled in circles above them.

One day the hunter is out chasing a deer. This implies that he has left the proximity of his home in order to follow the deer. In so doing, he is also subject to new influences. In fairy tales, stags and does tend to lure the protagonists into the realm of the otherworldly, to a place where they have to either defend themselves valiantly or succumb. They are seduced into the heart of the problem. The deer is the sacred animal of the birth goddess.[26] A fleeing deer can express the idea of longing, a sentiment that one may not yet be able to articulate oneself, a feeling of being ineluctably drawn to the unknown. Lurking behind this might well be the influence of the birth goddess Artemis herself, since something is on the verge of a major transformation. The fleeing deer unleashes the impulse to shoot and to possess it. The impulse is so overwhelming that the hunter pursues the deer obsessively. Indeed, he is so preoccupied with his quarry that he does not notice that he has strayed into the proximity of the dreaded pond. The thrill of the chase has so captivated him that he must bag the deer, no matter what the cost. Although it does seem that his desire might be extinguished with the killing of the deer, it nonetheless leads him to the source of his longing, namely to the nixie. He now "has" his deer. He has pursued it with all his heart. And this is just the kind of sexual-erotic image that is current—and one which says a lot about the relationship between the sexes. By this he probably also thinks that he "has" the nixie— that he has incorporated into his life whatever it is that the nixie embodies. This, however, is not the case. It is just the opposite way around: the nixie in fact "has" him. He has been possessed by a psychological reality which makes him extremely vulnerable, yet this is not something that occurs to him. While he is washing his bloody hands in the water, the nixie rises up out of the pond, gives a laugh, and envelops

him with her wet arms. Then she draws him down to
the bottom. It is not a demonic nixie that awaits him,
but an enthusiastic one, a laughing and perhaps
rather triumphant figure. Apparently, the hunter has
nothing with which to fight her.

Having been so thoroughly gripped by passion, he
falls completely under her spell. The fairy tale needs
to express the idea that he likes finding himself in the
arms of the nixie at the bottom of the pond.

The bloody act is necessary for the hunter to sustain life. According to Walter Burkert,[27] hunting peo-
ples who have been studied from an ethnological
point of view often experienced feelings of guilt with
regards to their quarry. Associated with these feelings
were rituals of recompense. Burkert interprets this to
mean that the experience of violent death is a central
one. The "bloody 'act' was a necessary part of life.
Indeed, it was not made less necessary by virtue of the
fact that new life comes into being."[28] In the practice
of hunting, both aggression and sexuality come into
play: aggression between men is directed at animals.
While the hunter is going about his business, he must
renounce his own sexual gratification, since the
undertaking demands that all powers be channelled
into the hunt.

Burkert mentions the point that although the act
of killing might be sexually charged, sexual abstinence is often part of the preparation for the hunt. He
recalls Hippolytos who was in the service of Artemis
and for whom abstinence had become an "unrenoun-
cable way of life. By the same token, his demise

signified Aphrodite's triumph, and his grave and shrine are marked by a temple to Aphrodite."[29]

It is in the death of the hunter's prey, and particularly in the spilling of blood, that the human being's resemblance to the animal is most recognizable.[30] The hunter feels guilty and, as a result, his willingness to give recompense grows. He recognizes that he has overstepped a boundary, and the sacrificial meal celebrates this desire for recompense. Killing and the threat of death correspond in equal measure; in causing death, death itself is made possible, repeatable, and conquerable through the celebratory meal.[31]

However, it is this very ritual which does not take place in our fairy tale. Ultimately, death is not just handed to the hunter. This is probably the lesson he has to learn. In the event that he thought he could do whatever he wanted, then he must learn that this is no longer the case. And this is where the nixie triumphs. In his sexual abstinence and exclusive concentration on the act of killing, the hunter has probably grown more and more sure of his own prowess. He may even have grown convinced of his capacity to triumph over death and the metamorphosis that necessarily ensues. Yet now, he is in the hands of the nixie. He has to learn a new lesson. The birth goddess teaches that in spite of death, life achieves continuity through births and not through an overidentification with death as the indestructible destroyer.[32]

The theme of love and death becomes ever clearer. He has experienced passion. This is most clearly expressed in the inexorable pursuit of the deer, as well as in the image of his bloody hands which makes the business of killing so graphic. He has also been confronted with vitality and the loss of vitality, and he has thus become vulnerable. Now death is brought into focus—he cannot simply erase the fear of death and overcome the fear of losing everything he holds dear by killing. He has to learn to go through this painful process and submit himself to the realm of the nixie.

In the Arms of the Nixie at the Bottom of the Pond

Whatever we might imagine, the hunter's disappearance means that the link with his wife is broken; the two are separated, and the wife experiences this as a desperate loss, which in effect determines what happens next in the story. What he feels we do not know. One could guess, though, that the hunter has been seized by a passion so strong that he forgets all about normal life. It might also be that he falls into a deep depression, for the very reason that he cannot transfer this passion to the marriage with his wife—that the passion is simply unrealizable. One could also imagine that the nixie is projected onto a real woman who is perhaps more "hot-blooded" than his wife. Whatever the scenario, the promise that the miller once made has now been fulfilled. The nixie has the thing that she demanded.

A man who is attracted to nixies and who has inherited this preoccupation from his father suffers from an inability to experience deep emotions, sensuality, and love. However, he can control this attraction and the implicit danger for a protracted length of time if he employs certain avoidance strategies. Among these avoidance strategies is the notion of being someone who can do whatever he wants. But at some point, all the attempts to compensate fall apart, and the object of fear has to be confronted. Our longings often lead us to the very things that frighten us. However, what frightens us is also what attracts us, the thing that can lead us to new life experiences, to an abundance of life if only we can develop the courage to confront it.

A Time of Mourning

In the evening, the hunter did not come home from his hunting, and his wife grew afraid. She went out looking for him, but since he had always told her that he had to be careful that the nixie did not get him and that he could not go anywhere near the pond, she soon guessed what had happened to him. She hurried to the water's edge, and when she found his hunting pouch lying on the bank, she was no longer in doubt as to what had happened. Wringing her hands and crying out in grief, she called the name of her beloved, but in vain. She ran to the opposite side of the pond and called to him again. She hurled curses at the nixie but received no answer. The water's surface was as smooth as a mirror, and the face of the crescent moon looked up at her without so much as a blink.

The poor woman refused to leave the pond. With anxious steps and without pausing for a moment, she went round and round the pond. Sometimes she was silent, sometimes she let out a powerful scream, and

*then again gave a little whimper. Finally, her strength
was at an end: she sank down onto the ground and fell
into a deep sleep. Before long she started to dream.*

For the most part, the continuation of the fairy tale is
now left up to the hunter's wife. For this reason, I am
now going to turn my attention to her and look at her
attempts to rescue the hunter as the actions of a
woman who, in a comparable life situation, would try
to reinstate her relationship with the person she
loved. As long as her husband was a hunter, she barely had any role to play. Now, however, she becomes
the main protagonist.

When the hunter fails to return home, his wife
becomes very frightened. She knows what the threat
is, and she guesses what has happened. When she sees
his hunting pouch lying on the bank of the pond, it
is all too clear. She expresses her feelings about her
loss. Crying out in grief, she calls the name of her
beloved; she wants to have him back. She curses the
nixie, but it is all in vain. *"The water's surface was as
smooth as a mirror, and the face of the crescent moon
looked up at her without so much as a blink."* Nothing
stirs, she sees the moon not in the sky but perceives
it reflected on the surface of the water. Instead of
relinquishing her husband, the water shows her the
image of the crescent moon. It is a half-moon—perhaps a symbol of the fact that in suffering the loss of
her husband, she only feels half herself. Or rather, it
may be a symbol of the fact that in the process of
accessing her femininity, she initially feels only half

of what there is to feel. We do not know, after all, if the moon is half full or half empty.

In the story, the moon and its phases are introduced. By virtue of the fact that the moon constantly changes, it has become a symbol of constant metamorphosis. As such, cyclical lunar time has come to be associated with birth (new moon to full moon) and death (full moon to no moon)—and thus also with rebirth. The three phases of the moon—new, waxing (full), old (new or dark moon)—are also associated with the threefold goddess: the goddess as young girl, the goddess as mature woman, and the goddess as wise old woman who knows the secrets of death. With its influences on the earth, the sea, and the female being, the moon is often associated with the female cycle and fertility, and thus also with woman as a whole. The image of a half-moon is a common one when it comes to representing the moon symbolically. Depicted as a sickle, the moon represents an attribute of virgin goddesses like Artemis. The full moon, on the other hand, is linked to the theme of pregnancy and birth. Thus, the hunter's wife must now undergo a transformation and, in so doing, develop into a mature woman who is capable of bearing children. Apparently, it then is easier for her to deal with the problem of the nixie, even though this is by no means an easy task. It is a necessary reaction arising from the situation in which she finds herself.

Although there is little hope that anything will change, the woman circles the pond. At times, she cries out in anguish, wringing her hands; at other times, she is quiet and whimpers in pain. She grieves. This is a new emotion and a new way of behaving in this fairy tale. When he suffered a loss, the miller grew depressed. Up until this point in the story, no one has gone through the process of grief. However, grief is the emotion through which we express our feelings of loss over something that was very valuable to us. Grief is also an emotion that we can give ourselves over to, as we see in the case of the hunter's wife. It is an emotion that helps us to work through our pain so that we become capable of starting a new life in spite of the loss we have suffered. At first the hunter's wife does not want to believe what she really knows has happened, namely that she has lost her husband to the nixie. She is in a state of denial, having retreated behind the barrier we always erect when something shocks us very deeply. However, when she sees her husband's hunting pouch and she cannot deny the facts any longer then, she starts to cry and to curse the nixie, saying that she wants her husband back. This is just the way that people grieve when they have lost someone they love. They cry and curse fate, which in this instance is embodied in the form of the nixie who has intervened in their lives. The image of the moon on the surface of the water could offer some hope—it is after all a half-moon, and even if it will first disappear again, it is still half full. However, this is a sign of hope that the woman cannot take in, cannot perceive. She circles the pond—circles the problem of her loss—and in so doing, she sees the problem from all possible perspectives. She does this until she cannot go on. In speaking of the grieving process, one would describe this as passing out of the phase of denial and into one characterized by the "outbreak of chaotic emotions."[33]

When all her strength leaves her—this expression of emotion calls for an enormous amount of energy— she drops to the ground and falls into a deep sleep. She relinquishes the burden she has been carrying to the earth and to sleep. In so doing, she gives herself over to something that envelops her, something that for at least a little while takes away her pain. From the point of view of conscious action, she has done all that there is to do. She has no power left with which to mourn. One could almost say that she has grieved aggressively; she certainly has taken an active role in mourning. Now, she gives herself over to a physical state of being and to her own unconscious. It is under these circumstances that she has a dream.

As a result of her crisis and her doubt, she has expressed her feelings so openly that she has no defense mechanisms left with which to repress or con-trol her feelings. She is in close proximity to her unconscious, which in this sort of situation is often expressed by the appearance of a significant dream. In crisis situations—and of course the experience of loss is a crisis situation—dreams tend to deal in a very spe-cific way with the problem at hand. The reason for this is that the person has almost no defense mecha-nisms. As a result of the dream, something happens to the hunter's wife that happens to many people in cri-sis situations: help comes in the form of a dream.[34]

The Dream

Before long she started to dream.

Fearfully, she climbed up a hill strewn with huge boulders; thorns and brambles pricked her feet, the rain fell on her face, and the wind whipped her long hair. When she reached the top, there was altogether another view to behold. The sky was blue, the air mild, and the grass undulated gently. In the midst of a green field bedecked with colorful wildflowers, there stood a little hut. She went up to the hut and opened the door. There sat an old woman with white hair who gave her a friendly wave. At that moment, the poor woman awoke. Daylight had long since broken, and she decided to follow the dream's bidding. With great effort, she climbed up the hill and everything was just as it had been in the dream. The old woman received her with open arms and offered her a chair to sit on. "You must have suffered a terrible misfortune," she said, "if you have taken it upon yourself to search out my lonely hut." Crying all the while, the woman told her what had happened. "Take heart, my dear," said the old woman. "I want to help you. You have in your hair a golden comb. Wait until the full moon rises, then go down to the pond. Seat yourself on the bank and comb your long black hair with the comb. When you are finished combing your hair, lay the comb down on the bank and you will see what happens next."

The woman went home to wait, but the days until the full moon passed very slowly. At long last, the luminous disk appeared in the sky, and the woman went down to the pond. She sat herself down and combed her long black hair with the golden comb. When she was finished, she laid the comb down at the water's edge. It was not long before the depths began to stir. A wave appeared; it rolled up onto the bank and lapped up the comb. Before long, the comb sank to the bottom of the pond, and with this, the mirrorlike surface of the water parted and the hunter's head appeared above the surface. He did not speak, but simply looked sadly at his wife. At the very same moment, a second wave rolled in and covered the man's head. Everything disappeared. The pond lay as peaceful and undisturbed as before. Only the face of the full moon glimmered on the surface.

Disconsolate, the woman returned home, and just as before, a dream came to her in which she saw the hut of the old woman. The next morning, she again set off for the old woman's hut, and she told her of her sorrow. The old woman gave her a golden flute and said, "Wait until the full moon comes again, then take this flute and seat yourself on the bank of the pond. Play a pretty tune on the flute and when you are finished lay it on the sand. Then you will see what happens next."

The woman did what the old woman had bidden her.
Barely had she placed the flute on the sandy bank, when
the depths began to stir. A wave rolled in and lapped up the
flute. Hereupon, the waters parted, and there appeared not
just the hunter's head but half his body too. He spread out
his arms in longing, but a second wave rolled in, covered
him in water, and carried him to the bottom of the pond.

Fearfully, the woman climbed up the hill. Her fear is
emphasized, but at the same time things are on the
upswing, despite the fact that there are a few "rocks"
in the way, rocks that she has to get around. The
route that she clearly has to take is thorny. All kinds
of things try and trip her up and make it likely that
she will fall. But it is not only the path that is thorny,
a symbol of what she has to endure at the moment; to
make things worse, it is also raining, and the wind
blasts her face. In the most literal sense of the word,
she has to make her way through a head wind which
whips her long hair. The whole image conveys the
tremendous effort that she has to exert in order to get
to the top. However, pitting herself against the
onslaught means ascending into a realm that reveals
entirely other aspects of life. At the top, the weather
is calm, and it is unbelievably beautiful. On a green
meadow, there stands a little hut. Here everything is
very orderly and conducive to trust. The color green
seems to predominate. It is a color that suggests
growth and a state of becoming—and in this instance,
it also suggests hope. The young woman opens the

door and sitting there is an old woman with white hair who gives her a friendly wave. The old woman greets her in a friendly manner, happy that the wife of the hunter has opened the door of her hut. The dream ends with the hope that the path would lead to this old woman[35] and that she might have some advice for the young woman.

And at this moment, with hope awakened, the young woman herself wakes up, and she decides to do just what the dream has bidden her do. After all, in the dream, she did get so far as to open the door of the old woman's hut, and she was brave enough to step over the threshold. Whether out of despair, hope, or just some leftover tenacity, she follows her dream. This proves to be a difficult undertaking, just as the dream foretold. Nonetheless, she finds the old woman, also as promised, and the old woman offers her a chair. In other words, the old woman invites her to stay there at least for a while. By offering her a chair, the old woman lets her know that she recognizes what a tremendous effort it has taken to get here.

The old woman now approaches her in a very similar fashion to the way the nixie approached the miller: the old woman addresses her unhappiness and brings her to speak about her problems. Over and over again in the fairy tale, we are told how important it is for us to tell other people what is bothering us.

The wise old woman could be someone who has sought out the young woman, after she herself has fought her way alone through the dense undergrowth of emotions and thoughts with only hope to spur her

on, the hope that things will improve and that someone will come to her aid. On the other hand, the wise
old woman can also be regarded as an aspect of the
young woman's psyche, an aspect which comes to the
fore when she no longer knows which way to turn and
has all but given up. At such times, we find that there
is a voice in us that does have some suggestions after
all. Against our better judgment, we find that there is
some hope; we are in contact with some wise part of
ourselves that comes from within, but that also transcends us, something that seems much older than we
in fact are. The dream was already an expression of
this spiritual wisdom. But the fact that the young
woman is prepared to follow the dream means that
she is already at least somewhat familiar with the old
woman and trusts her.

The Wise Woman[36]

The wise old woman, and the wise woman in general, is a figure that appears often in fairy tales. She is not, however, always called the "wise woman" or the "wise old woman." She might appear as an old woman whom the hero or heroine encounters when he or she set off to solve the problem that has been presented.[37] These old women demand polite treatment; they want to take part in a meal, to be wined and dined. As an aside, they might inquire about the why and the wherefore of the hero's journey, give advice and a magical object that will help the hero when the going gets rough. Having done this, they disappear again. They set the hero or the heroine on the way; they ask the most important questions as a way of orienting the protagonist and getting him or her to concentrate on the task at hand. Aside from this, they link the present moment with the question of why they have been set the task in the first place.

In other words, they link the past with the future. And above all, they give a piece of advice that has to be followed in some way or other. The hero and hero-ine must themselves be wise enough to be able to rec-ognize wisdom in whatever decrepit form it presents itself along the way. And of course, he or she has to realize that it is worthwhile heeding the advice of the wise old man or woman.

The wise old woman also appears in instances in which the hero or heroine comes into conflict with a demonic figure. An example of this would be the fairy tale, "The Devil with the Three Golden Hairs."[38] In this story, the devil's grandmother is very obliging, and she outwits the devil on behalf of the hero. By this, I mean that she is not just a cunning grand-mother—although she is this too. She is wise because she knows how the world works. She understands how to set the hero on his own course in life and, in so doing, helps him save his life. Incidentally, she does this without wanting anything from him for herself. In other fairy tales, the wise old woman is sometimes called "granny." Granny Evergreen,[39] for example, keeps an eye on a sick mother's children, checking to see whether they have a good heart on not—and it is only if they are good-hearted that they get the medi-cine that their mother so urgently needs.

Quite often, the wise old woman appears as a herbalist. She is not necessarily called "wise" in this kind of fairy tale. Instead, she may be deemed disre-spectable, like the old beggar woman in the Norwegian fairy tale Zottelhaube, for example.[40] What she then suggests, however, is enormously wise. She knows all about the curative properties of different plants. Above all, she knows what the king and queen should do in order to cure the problem of infertility that has plagued them so long. In fairy tales, the herbalist is particularly interested in questions related to childbearing and, at times, also in the problem of bringing the dead back to life.

Frequently, the wise old woman also appears as presiding over an initiation ritual. Examples of this would include "Mrs. Holle," "The Goosegirl at the Fountain,"[41] and "With the Black Woman."[42] The wise woman initiates the young girl into life as a woman and to the possibility of having children. It is also not uncommon for these wise women to have a thoroughly dark side pent up within them. And this can make them be absolutely dastardly.

In the fairy tale that we are dealing with, the woman is called both old and wise. She helps the young woman establish her erotic relationship, or reestablish it, she initiates her into erotic-sexual life. Like all wise women in fairy tales, she takes her on because she is in need, because she is being buffeted by the vagaries of life. As is the preserve of these wise old women, she gives some advice, yet sends the young woman on her own way. This is what is perhaps typical of all these wise women: they give some advice, but they do not accompany the heroine. Nonetheless, in this fairy tale, the old woman obviously waits for the heroine. She sits there in the same place, waiting patiently.

These wise women are inextricably linked to springs, plants, and animals. They spin wool and guard the fire, they cook, and as herbalists, they heal people and prepare intoxicants. In other words, ultimately they are concerned with the question of inspiration. It is also not difficult to see in them an aspect of the great goddess who intervenes in order to give advice and make a life situation viable again. The wise old woman is also like the nixie. She knows so much about the nixie that we can assume that she embodies an older version of the nixie and is not simply a goddess. She is one of those figures who can appear in our dreams without conveying to us the impression that we have been visited by a goddess. She is a figure upon whom we can rely, whom we can experience at a spiritual level, and who can help us realize our fantasies. And yet nonetheless, it is the great goddess who is at the source of all this.

When the wise old woman appears in dreams or the imagination, then women feel comforted; they are seized by a new feeling of hope, they sense that they do indeed have the strength to cope and to set themselves on course again. But above all, they realize that life is not falling apart, that it has meaning. They also come to see that they have spiritual powers that can lead the way to a more sensual way of life. Just when things are looking really hopeless, when there is no way out, and life seems desperate, then the old woman intervenes. The experience of being in the most difficult of life situations and suddenly discovering strengths and ideas that we did not think we

had is a common human experience. However, part
of this involves leaving oneself open to such experiences. In this fairy tale, the young woman opens the
door to the old woman, she steps inside, and she
opens herself up to hearing what it is that the old
woman has to say. She steps into a space that is the
preserve of the wise old woman.

The Wise Old Woman in the Crisis of a Modern Woman

A thirty-eight-year-old woman has lost her partner, someone with whom she has spent the last eighteen years of her life. The death of her partner in an automobile accident has plunged her into profound grief. In actual fact, she would not have minded dying too. But there were the children to think about, and she felt totally responsible for them. So she forced herself to live on, but felt as though she were "frozen." She was convinced that she would never be able to enjoy life again.

To make matters worse, at the age of eight she had lost her father in an automobile accident as well. She was not really aware of what the loss of her father might have meant for her at this age, but she did know that she had loved him very much and missed him for a long, long time. The more recent loss seemed to now plunge her into a double grief. Coupled with memories of her partner came the memories of her father as well. She felt as though she had been doubly deprived. Because the woman thought her grief might do the children some harm, she decided to seek therapeutic help.

Three months after the beginning of therapy, she had a dream which deeply affected her: *"I am in an inaccessible, rocky area. Suddenly, I see my partner emerging from a pond. I see his pleading eyes. Then he disappears in the water again; he leaves me alone. I wake up bathed in tears."*

By way of an initial reaction, the woman said that she was very angry about the dream. She said that the dream told her only what she already knew, namely that her husband had disappeared out of her life, and aside from this, she had now been plunged into renewed despair. And yet, although she was now sadder than before, she was happy to see her partner again. "For a moment, it was as though he had come back into my life again; for a moment, everything was as it used to be."

Then for quite some time, she spoke about the pleading, begging eyes of her partner. Because the woman liked having seen her husband again, and because his pleading eyes had made such an impression on her, I got the impression that this dream could provide an insight that the woman, and the two of us, had not had before. I decided to use the imagination technique[43] as a way of working with the dream. The woman had already used the technique on occasion, and in some ways, she was quite talented when it came to both taking her fantasies seriously and working on herself. After a few relaxation exercises, I asked her to go through the dream again and to describe in as much detail as possible the feelings that corresponded to the images she was conjuring up.

Her imagination: *"I am in this closed off, inaccessible landscape. It is gray and foggy. There are bushes and rocks all over the place. I feel very alone and vulnerable in these wild surroundings. I don't see any paths leading away from this place; there is no opening. It is as though I am locked in. The only option would be to fly out. But how would a plane find its way here?"*

I asked her to concentrate on the pond again: *"I am not sure if it is a pond or a hole in the ground—a bomb crater, perhaps. My partner emerges out of it, so whatever it is, there is water in it. Actually, it is amazing that there is water around at all. So there must be an opening—an opening in the ground."*

Having said this, she let out a sigh and visibly relaxed. She seemed to feel a bit better once she had realized that there was in fact a way out of her current psychological situation, even if this way out was "down below." Clearly, she did not see the open sky above her. After crying quietly to herself for a while, she returned to her inner images and said: *"I now see how my partner emerges from the water. His face is really desperate, and he looks at me again with these pleading eyes. I can see his eyes very clearly, and it feels as though I'm really in touch with him. It is almost like a real meeting.* (Her breathing became noticeably quicker). *He wants me to forgive him for having died. Or should I just forgive him period? But forgive him for what?"*

With this, the anger that she had been feeling but not dared express was suddenly transferred to her husband. She was angry that her husband had left her, especially when she needed him so much, and she was also angry with her father. She expressed these feelings, and when after a little while she had calmed down, she decided to look into her partner's eyes once again: *"He's still looking at me, not reproachfully, but as though he wants something from me. I think I can forgive him—at least for today. I have a good feeling. It's done me good to feel my anger and let it all out. Actually, I think that my anger doesn't have a whole lot to do with him. But when I look at him, his face seems more peaceful. Perhaps now I can let him go more easily."*

Then, quite clearly surprised, she added the following: *"Now I see myself in this pond. My partner is no longer anywhere to be seen. I am sad and confused. Why isn't he there any more? I call him. I want him back. But death doesn't listen. At least, I want to have him in my imagination, in my fantasies, like I did just now. But I can't do it anymore. This is crazy. I just can't get it to work now. I'm really disappointed, oh, I feel so horribly sad. I just feel like going to sleep. I am so exhausted."*

Having said this, the woman sat all crumpled up in her chair. She seemed absolutely exhausted, but reiterated in a very soft voice, as though to remind herself, that what she had experienced in this exercise was very important. It provided a way out of the problem. Something opened up inside her when she released her anger and expressed her feelings. She found it really strange that she could not conjure him up in her imagination any more. But then she said to herself, "I can't and don't want to spend the rest of my life looking into my dead partner's eyes."

The dream signaled a transition in the grieving process. The woman was moving out of what I call "the phase of chaotic emotions" and into the third phase, that of searching, finding, and letting go, and the real work of grieving. In order to reach this stage, it is important to express the rage that is associated with the loss that has occurred. Up until this point, the woman had not expressed any feelings of anger. She also had to become aware that she was thoroughly fixated on her dead partner, and that she was only dealing with him. The dream that she had had was the beginning of her coming to grips with the fact that death had brought the relationship to an end. This period usually begins with the person saying that she cannot think about anything other than the person who has died. What normally happens next is that she wants someone to intervene so that she can put an end to this state of affairs. This does not help, however, since the person who is grieving has to think about the one she has lost and to let her fantasies about their life together surface. It is only then that she can start to let go. My client actively tried to forget her partner so that she could think about other things. The more she tried to forget, the more he subconsciously took over her thoughts. As a result, she came across as being very rigid and hemmed in. What the dream and our exercise clearly showed was that the only way out of this restrictive situation was through a confrontation with her partner. At the end of the therapy session, my client looked completely exhausted and discouraged. I thought again about the images that she had described. Suddenly, I remembered the fairy tale, "The Mermaid in the Pond." It seemed to me that this fairy tale could contribute something to her understanding of the dream and the exercise we had done. At the very least, I thought she might be able to put them into some larger, more visceral context.

I told her about the fairy tale, but only about the part that corresponded to her dream and what she had brought up in the exercise. I related how the desperate woman ran around the pond, cursing the nixie, and how, when she was completely at her wit's end, she dropped down exhausted and fell into a deep sleep. I told her about the dream, about the appearance of the old woman and the gifts that she gave which little by little enabled the nixie to relinquish the hunter. I told her about how he kept appearing out of the water, only to disappear again.

In therapeutic terms, the introduction of fairy-tale images constitutes a form of countertransference.[44] The fairy-tale images are images that the therapist conjures up. They arise as a result of the therapist's relationship to the client's subconscious and are possibly the product of both subconsciouses.[45] This form of countertransference is a creative impulse. It enables personal material that has some comparable imagery (and which some people can find very powerful and evocative) to be introduced as a way of putting things into a larger context. If this sort of elaboration came at the right moment—if in other words, my client could make some use of these images—then the fairy tale could incorporate her images into a developmental process that might lead to a solution of her problem. This after all is the great advantage of fairy stories: they locate symbols and symbolic configurations that we know from dreams and imaginative exercises within psychic processes. They give an implicit sense of hope that the problem which has been expressed through the dream can be solved. Because they are not concrete suggestions per se, they provide possible solutions that do not have to be taken literally. Instead, they convey the idea that despite the way things are, a solution is possible after all. The hope that the person feels is accompanied by a burst of energy. The dream and fantasy are in other words, enriched by fantasies that have always moved people, and which are thus always retold in stories.

My client listened attentively to what I had to say as I told her the part of the story that I just related. Then she asked me to tell her the rest of the fairy story. I gave her a brief summary, but also told her that I did not have the impression that the fairy story could be applied as a whole to her situation. I told her that what had struck me was the similarity of the "pond images." Then I mentioned again, only this time in more detail, the images of desperation and those of hope which the fairy tale described.

In the next therapy session, she decided to "fantasize" about the images expressed in the fairy tale. She wanted to find out whether these images correlated with her own experience. They did indeed. In the first phase of the exercise, she felt very close to the hunter's wife. She saw the images in the fairy tale from her own point of view. In sympathy with the hunter's wife she felt desperate, and then she too generated a new feeling of hope: *"I experienced these images as though they were my own. That made me happy. It suddenly became clear to me that I also have a strong desire to survive. In my imagination, I have discovered the strength with which I fight against adversity, against the undergrowth, against the stones, against the rain. I have really come to feel my vitality again. Perhaps I can think about these images again when I am at home, when I feel as though I'm about to lapse into that terrible feeling of apathy."*

In the second phase of the exercise, at the client's request I read the text of the fairy tale again. This time, I read from the part where the hunter's wife first makes an appearance up to the part that goes, "You must have experienced some misfortune if you have sought out my lonely hut." Then I was silent, and after a short pause the client continued the story. However, the story that she told was no longer that of the fairy tale, but rather her own story. With great animation, she projected herself onto the hunter's wife and described the experience of loneliness, desperation, and the unsatisfiable longing for erotic and sexual encounters. Unexpectedly, she told the old woman stories about her life together with her partner, about the life that had been brought to such an abrupt end. She told her about their joys, their grievances, their worries and fears. She experienced the wise old woman as being really ancient, white-haired, and smelling of dry pine cones, just like the memory of her great-grandmother whom she had known as a small child. In talking to the wise old woman, she managed to work through a lot of grief. She struggled to find out what the relationship with her partner had meant to her. She tried to find out what qualities he had evoked in her, what parts of her he had animated. Above all, she wanted to discover a way of introducing into her current life some of the aspects of the life that she had shared with her partner.

This conversation with the old woman helped to unburden my client. It gave her some reassurance that she would not have to continue to live in this isolated, gray, and stony wasteland—which was the image of her current predicament that she had conjured up for herself. This "conversation" was followed by others. In the exercises that we did together, she always sought out the old woman's hut. Each time, the journey grew a little easier, except on those days when she was not doing as well, and the path up to the old woman's hut then became difficult once again. Each time she spoke with the old woman and the old woman listened, I, as therapist, had the task of listening to them both. After these exercises, my client needed me to reaffirm the most important points and to contemporize what she had said, particularly at those times when the really "big" things seemed to be slipping away from her.

These exercises using the fairy tale effected her mood. She felt a little less pressured, she also became more active, and she saw a change in the kind of dreams she had been having. By way of example, I could mention the following dream: *"I'm washing my body and, in so doing, wash off my skin a substance that feels kind of like dry clay. I can peel off great big flakes of the stuff, big pieces, and with every bit that I peel off, I feel freer. It's like exhaling."*

This motive of liberation in the dream speaks for itself. In her conversation with the old woman, my client spoke about what a great feeling it was, it was as though she were shedding an old skin. One could interpret this shedding of a skin to mean that as a result of her grief, the woman regressed: she became clothed in a clay skin, as in an archetypal placenta, which she was able to slough off through the process of grieving. As a result, she emerged as though born anew.

In hearing this fairy tale, the client recognized an aspect of the story and made it into her own reality: a woman who has suffered a loss must make use of all her strengths in order to come into contact with the wise old woman in her own psyche: by establishing contact with her, the woman achieves a feeling of comfort and security. The client managed to attain this state because she was able to relate her dream motives to a well-known fairy story. In so doing, it also became clear to her that loss and death are part of an eternal problem, a problem for which human beings have always sought the answer. She came to see that human beings have always had to reconcile themselves to loss and have had to learn to live on in spite of death. The images inspired by the fairy story conjured up useful images in the woman's psyche. By focusing on the collective images and the collective imaginative process, she was able to draw some strength and take heart.[46]

The Advice Given by the Old Woman in the Fairy Tale

The young woman uses a golden comb and combs her hair by the light of the moon while sitting at the edge of the pond. When she is finished, she is supposed to lay the comb down by the water's edge. Repeatedly she is told, "And you will see what happens next."

The nixie also has long hair. And people say, among other things, that the nixie combs her hair in order to lure men to her. The combing of long hair is a form of erotic behavior. It also demonstrates, however, that the nixie has a proud awareness of her ability to be seductive. She knows that she is capable of arousing passion and desire.[47] In other words, the young woman is supposed to do what nixies are said to do. In a less conscious way, she is supposed to behave like a nixie, to comb her hair with a golden comb.

Besides this, it becomes clear that the old woman even has a nixie's comb in her possession, and since it is made of gold, it is indestructible. This is clear evidence that the old woman was also a nixie once upon a time. But what could be the purpose of encouraging the young woman to behave a bit like a nixie?

If we examine the fairy tale from the point of view of couple dynamics, then it can be assumed that both the hunter and the young woman suffer from a "nixie problem." This could mean that the young woman might have had something of the seductive nixie in her, but that she has thoroughly repressed this aspect of herself. She may have tried to become a real "anti-nixie" because her husband was frightened of her seductive qualities. In altering her behavior, she would have enabled her husband to feel secure. She would never have elicited powerful feelings in him, feelings which may have made him feel as though he did not know who he was. Yet for all this, the feelings of longing just have to be satisfied elsewhere.

The issue here is that a woman is considered so seductive that she has to repress some aspect of herself. In addition to this, the problem has become a collective one, whereby the nixie (who is after all, the great goddess) is excluded from life. As a result, the nixie problem effects all women, and the task is to reincorporate what has been repressed into our everyday lives. At least, this is the advice that the wise old woman gives. She says that this combing of the hair should take place at the time of the full moon. We should bare in mind that the young woman has lost her husband at the time of the half-moon. The full moon would be the time of female fullness, it would be the time when something achieves a state of completion, a time when a woman could be particularly seductive. This would also suggest a momentary maturation and a state of complete womanhood.

When it is finally the time of the full moon, the young woman does as the old woman has advised. When she lays the comb down at the water's edge, a wave rolls up and fetches it away. One could say that in exchange for the comb, the mirrored surface of the water parts and the hunter's head becomes visible. It is a strange situation: he does not speak, he just looks sadly at his wife. And for her part, she stands on the bank, she can see him but cannot reach him or touch him. This only lasts a moment and then a second wave washes the image away, and all is calm again around the pond: *"The face of the full moon was reflected on the surface."* The beauty of the image stands in curious contrast to the desperate situation of longing, being unable to reach one another, and the ensuing grief on the part of the hunter and his wife.

What is depicted here is clearly an expression of the third phase of grief, the phase in which the real business of grieving starts to occur. In this phase, the person who is grieving tries to conjure up the person she has lost and to make the person as real as possible in her own psyche. This phase involves memory; it implies the withdrawal of the projections that the person has made and the delegating that she has done; it means becoming aware of the deeper levels of the soul that were animated by the relationship and finding a way of not letting go of these qualities once the relationship has come to an end. And most difficultly, at the same time that the dead person is being conjured up so vividly, the person who is grieving tries to let this person go, since he is after all dead.

Some people do not want to do this grief work—and hard work it certainly is—because they say: Why should I conjure up memories of my beloved if I am to then going to just lose him or her? They set about forgetting the person without remembering her. However, this results in the fact that no real letting go can take place. The fairy tale shows quite clearly the difficult combination of feelings that is associated with this grief work: there is the hope that one will encounter the person again, perhaps even a feeling of attraction; there is the feeling that everything could be the way it once was, and at the same time, there is the feeling of the most profound disappointment, the shift from hope to abject hopelessness, and the renewed experience of loss. In this instance, what we are dealing with is a particular kind of grief: we know that ultimately the young woman will win her husband back. In other words, the story is about a grief situation in which a separation takes place, one that is also reversible. This is made clear insofar as, in experiencing this grieving phase, the woman does not just go through the feelings associated with grief, she also develops some of the qualities associated with the nixie. Most people do develop as a result of the grieving process. Here, however, it has to do with a grieving process associated with a sense of alienation from one's beloved. As such, what is called for is a process of psychological development that deals with the basic problem in the relationship. The couple has to deal with the problem which has led to the alienation in the first place and caused them in varying degrees to suffer.[48] All we know is that the woman wants to get her husband back, and this is something that the old woman also knows, otherwise she would not have given the advice she did. She would have given her different suggestions. For the young woman who is in the midst of the grieving process, it would seem that all efforts are in vain.

How things seem to the husband is something we know much less about. The fact that we know little about him demonstrates that he can only be approached by way of fantasy. While the young woman is combing her hair, the fairy tale tells us that, *"He did not speak. He just looked at his wife sadly."* The second time we learn—and this is significant—that, *"Full of longing, he reached out his arms to her, but a wave rolled in, covered him over, and carried him down again."* He is incapable of establishing a verbal link. His expression shows that he is filled with longing, that he too wants to reestablish the connection, but we do not learn anything about his feelings of disappointment. They must be profound.

The fairy tale tells us that the young woman is beyond despair. She gets some comfort from her dream, which again shows her how to find the old woman's hut. And the next day, she makes her way there with renewed vigor. This time, she receives a golden flute that she must play by the light of the full moon.

Music, and above all singing, are the preserve of the nixie. With their gentle, mournful tunes they elicit the longing for feelings, for emotional spaces that extend beyond the everyday. They demonstrate their own longings; they express their feelings. At the same time, they also awaken a sense of emotional longing in those who hear them. In the sounds produced by the young woman's flute, which is comparable to the nixie's song, there is something otherworldly. The sounds evoke the longing for a link between this world and the next, between the here-and-now and the eternal. When the young woman plays her song, she demonstrates her very own melody, the progression that constitutes her own spiritual makeup; she exhibits her deepest, most sensitive feelings. In all likelihood, these feelings embody a sense of longing, love, grief, and the fact that she is cut off from the next world. It is also these feelings that enable her to respond to the love of another person. By playing this melody, the young woman more or less seduces the hunter out of the realm of the nixie. She also cultivates her capacity for expressing her feelings, and, in so doing, comes to resemble the nixie. At the same time, however, she expresses these feelings by means of a flute, which is something that is manmade. As a result, the hunter reappears in the water as far as his midriff. In the young woman's first attempt at seduction, only the hunter's head appeared. His eyes expressed everything, so that one might conclude that he was now capable of seeing his wife in a new way. The second time, however, one could imagine that the hunter not only sees the woman, but that his heart is also brought into play. He is now able to respond on a more emotional level. This happens in response to the fact that she too is addressing him in a very emotional, heartfelt way. But here too, she only sees a part of her husband. He is still a prisoner of the nixie. Nonetheless, he has become much more visible to her.

This is not however what she wants. She wants to be with him, to have all of him again. The experience of seeing him and immediately losing him again fills her with sorrow. She reacts in the same way as someone who is grieving who keeps "seeing" the person he or she has lost: conjuring up the person in the imagination, and yet knowing that ultimately she has to let him go.

The Conflict with
the Nixie

"**O**h, what is the good of being able to see my beloved if I am to keep losing him again?" asked the wretched woman. Her heart was filled with sorrow, and again the dream led her to the hut of the old woman. She set off again, and the wise old woman gave her a golden spinning wheel, comforted her, and said, "It is not complete yet. Wait until the full moon comes then take the spinning wheel and seat yourself on the bank and spin the spool full of wool. When you are finished, put the spinning wheel near the water and you will see what happens next."

The woman did everything exactly as she had been told. As soon as the full moon appeared, she carried the golden spinning wheel to the water's edge and spun busily until the flax was all gone and the spool was full of thread. Barely had she placed the spinning wheel on the bank, when something stirred in the depths more violently

than ever before. A powerful wave rushed past and car-
ried away the spinning wheel. Hereupon, a fountain of
water jetted the body of the man high into the air. Quickly
he leapt onto the bank and caught his wife's hand, and
they fled.

They had barely gone any distance, however, when the
entire pond rose with a terrible roar and flooded the entire
field. The fleeing couple saw their lives flash before their
eyes, and in fear, the wife called out to the old woman for
help. At that moment, they were transformed, she into a
toad and he into a frog. The flood that was lapping at their
feet could not drown them, but it tore them away from one
another and carried them far apart.

Once again, a dream conjures up the wise old woman
who offers some more advice. Whenever the sense of
despair gets the upper hand, then she appears. This
means that the young woman knows only too well
what she has to strive for if she is to be reunited with
her husband. With the next full moon, she must take
herself down to the pond and spin a ream of wool on
a golden spinning wheel.

It was Athena who invented spinning, weaving,
potting, but also the flute, the trumpet, the horse-
drawn carriage—and in fact, all the arts.[49] In other
words, the business of spinning is the preserve of several of the great goddesses. Among them, one of the
Greek goddesses of fate is called Klotho, the spinner.
It is she who spins the thread of life. Spinning is a
very regular activity, the spindle turns and turns. As
such, it is reminiscent of the eternal return of the

same. If one associates spinning with the spinning of the thread of fate, then the old woman probably means that the young woman has to try and find some sense of meaning in her fate. She has to try and make sense of the problem of the nixie and the loss she has experienced that is associated with this.

Spinning is not normally one of the activities associated with the nixie. These creatures have a more chaotic nature. If we take seriously the assertion that the nixie belongs to Artemis's retinue, then in the act of spinning, the young woman would also attempt to try to appropriate some aspect of the nixie. Quite possibly, she would attempt to remind the nixie of who she actually is—namely, also one of the great spinners. At the same time, however, it is also quite likely that in the past people have been so afraid of the nixie that they have downplayed and devalued some of her characteristics.

Spinning would mean bringing order out of chaos, creating a thread that one could then follow. And this is the very purpose of an encounter with the nixie: she introduces emotional chaos into life. This in turn ushers in new order and creates meaning, making it possible to spin the thread for as long as it takes to fill up the spool. This is just what the hunter's wife does, and in so doing, she emphasizes her great commitment to continuity. Thus, provided she just has a commitment to surviving, spinning could imply the introduction of a kind of order in the world of the nixie into the world of erotic-sexual attraction.

All repetitive activities such as spinning promote a psychological state conducive to dreaming and fantasy. When the woman spins by the light of the full moon, she might well fantasize about the possibilities of a new life with her husband. Perhaps she creates a picture for herself of how this future might look. After all, she has changed: she is now in touch with the nixie-like aspects of herself, as well as with the wise old woman. When the woman has these fantasies, then she believes her husband capable of liberating himself from his attraction to the nixie. She also trusts that she will be able to bring the nixie within herself to life. These sorts of fantasies cause the person who is conjuring them up to change: she becomes more hopeful; they also change the partner by trusting that he can free himself from the problematic clutches of the nixie and, by so doing, alter his whole life situation. In other words, the hunter can escape from the pond.

"Something stirred in the depths more powerfully than ever before." So says the fairy tale when the woman places the golden spinning wheel on the bank—a powerful psychic occurrence takes place, the elements are in an uproar. In conjunction with this enormous emotional upheaval, with the great uproar, is the husband's ejection from the pond. At first, it seems that everything will go well, but the pond "rises up with a terrible roar." It looks as though the dynamic embodied in the nixie is now expressed in the motion of the water. There is enormous power and a terrible rumbling. The fact that both of them

must flee demonstrates that the problem associated with the nixie is not at an end. They must flee her and her rage. For this reason, their first encounter after the great crisis is clearly under her sway: the two of them are "torn away" by a monstrous force, which is probably sexual passion. At the very moment in which they can take hold of one another again, they are overcome by the realm of the nixie.

Both of them suffer a regression, presumably at the moment they encounter one another sexually again. That the woman has established a link with the wise old woman is demonstrated by the fact that she is able to call on her in this life-threatening situation. In other words, she is not very far away—she has been incorporated into the young woman's psyche and, at the same time, can be understood as representing a kind of "fairy godmother" who is external to the young woman. The helping hand which comes to salvage this regression can only occur as a transformation, one which is in keeping with the situation: a toad and a frog can survive the flood. When the waters recede, then the two of them gain back their human forms—though they are separated.

Toads and frogs are animals which can survive on land as well as in the water. They are also animals which represent a transition. Because of their clearly visible stages of development—from the tadpole to toad or frog—they are hailed as symbols of transformation which embody several phases. The toad is linked to the moon and the principle of fertility, similarly the frog is also associated with the moon. In the negative sense, it represents an enslavement to the physical, and in the positive sense, a close connection with the fertility of the earth. Both animals point to transformation and fertility—they are linked to the uterus, and the frog can symbolize the soul of the unborn child.[50] Both symbolize the reawakening of life forces in the spring and summer and stand for an untrammeled desire to procreate. While the toad also has healing properties, the frog serves the purpose of enhancing love and fertility. These two symbols express the idea of an identification with the birth goddess at the animal level, and by implication, they imply the notion of great fertility.

Nonetheless, when the husband and wife encounter one another as frog and toad, then this has nothing to do with a personal encounter. It is symbolic of the fact that they have been torn apart by desire and a kind of archetypal dynamic that no individual can admit. They are also both very alike, since there is little difference between a frog and a toad. For this reason, they have to undergo a further process of separation, namely that of self-reflection. They have to live through the associated grieving process and change as a result. This coming together again as it is depicted in the story is typical of people who have been separated and then reunited. It is all too fast, too intense, too strongly determined by the emotions that belong to the realm of the nixie. For this reason, once the waters have subsided, the people involved completely lose sight of one another, and the separation is as radical as was the reunion.

A Time for Self-Protection

When the water had receded and both of them were on dry ground again, they metamorphosed back into the form of human beings. However, neither of them knew where the other one was. They found themselves among strangers who had never heard of their village. High mountains and deep valleys lay between them. In order to earn a living, they both had to tend sheep. For many years they drove their herds up hill and down dale, and were filled with sadness and longing.

When the water receded they were separated from each other by high mountains and deep valleys—they are among strangers. For many years they have to tend their herds, and they are full of sadness and longing.

They lose sight of one another and find themselves in a place in which they feel like strangers and must just concentrate on the business of shepherding. In fairy tales, being a shepherd is one of the lowliest of activities.

Both of them must now earn their own livelihood, and there is no one to take care of them. It is significant that the husband is no longer a hunter. Both are engaged in the same activity; both are now of a kind.

Shepherding is an activity in which one has to make sure one keeps together animals that would much rather go their own way. Taken symbolically, this could mean that one has to concentrate on collecting oneself, from both an internal and external point of view. One has to keep control of one's desires.

The situation in which the two of them now find themselves is a realm of life which is diametrically opposed to that of the nixie. In contradistinction to the untrammeled emotionality unleashed by the nixie, what has now been unleashed is the other emotional realm, the realm of concentrating on quiet feelings which are more easily associated with the relationship with the self. All of these realms are part of emotionality. People who thrive on untrammelled emotions and who like to let their feelings run away with them also have to cultivate the opposite realm, the emotions of concentrating and centering themselves.

Shepherds encircle their herds, or if it is not they who do so, then at least they have a dog that performs the function for them. We also have the gesture of encircling, of describing a circle which encloses and surrounds, making concentration possible. This is a very visual portrayal of focusing on the self, as we have already seen in the image of the grieving woman as she circled the pond. This time, however, both the husband and wife are engaged in the activity. If one circles round and round an issue, then one also gets to look at it from all different sides, and ultimately this creates a more balanced view of things. One also acquires a more balanced view of one's own life.

In the case of the two shepherds, of central concern are the feelings of longing and grief. In experiencing these emotions, both of them are busy concentrating on themselves. Grief can be associated with loss occasioned by death or separation or by a phase of inner separation[51] in which the partner is still around but the relationship has come to an end. In all of these instances, the grief process entails a more or less conscious focusing on the self and a reconception of what it means to exist as an independent individual. One has to become very aware of the things that one projected onto one's partner. Whatever aspects of life were delegated to them to take care of must now be retracted. One has to figure out what deep, unconscious images of being a couple were brought to life and actually enacted in the relationship. This process may well be taking place in the two shepherds if they are leading a lonely and self-sufficient existence tending their sheep. Since both belong to the same constellation, we might well compare the realm of the nixie with that of the wise old woman, even if they do embody different phases of the life-death thematic. In this case, the husband and wife find themselves predominantly in the realm of the wise old woman. They live under the archetype of the wise old woman and are dominated by the emotions of grief and longing.

Grief is the emotion that signals our loss of something that had great value to us. At the same time, it is the emotion which aids us in getting over the experience of loss. Longing is the emotion which allows us to envision the future. It shows us the new aspects of our psyche which will be brought to life and what new developmental stages are in store for us. Longing draws us into the as yet unlived phase of life and lets us anticipate life through our fantasy. Longing and grief intensify the experience of our own identity as an individual who would like to get involved with someone else. It makes us capable of getting on with life and opening ourselves up to other people.

This period of loneliness, longing, and grief can be interpreted as being a time in which the two lovers really are separated, but it can also be taken to mean a time of alienation in which they feel alone in the relationship. Feelings of alienation give expression to the fact that the intoxicating sexuality has rocked the foundations of their prior existence. Both of them have come to feel very threatened. As a frog and a toad, perhaps each feels incapable of dealing with the other on a personal level and just sees in the other the embodiment of a sexual being who is no longer the person with whom they had a psychological and spiritual relationship. Living in the shepherds' hut, however, they learn not only to be with themselves and how to relate to one another in a more rational way, but also how to exercise a certain solicitousness when it comes to life in general. They learn how to care for animals; they learn how to behave in a relational way, one that is characterized by care and attentiveness toward life and also toward their own bodies.

The Spring

One day when the first signs of spring were just appearing, both of them set out with their herds, and by a stroke of chance, they encountered one another. On a far-off mountainside, the man glimpsed another herd and set off with his sheep in that direction. They met in the valley but did not recognize one another. Nonetheless, they were happy not to be alone any more. From then on, they kept company, driving their herds together. Although they did not talk much, they nevertheless felt somehow comforted by one another's presence. One evening, when the full moon shone in the sky and the sheep were already asleep, the shepherd took a flute out of his bag and played a sad and beautiful tune. When he was done, he noticed that the woman was crying bitterly. "Why are you crying?" he asked her. "Oh," she sobbed, "the full moon was shining just like this the last time I played that song on my flute, and the body of my beloved emerged from the water." He looked at her closely, and it was as though the scales had *dropped from his eyes. He recognized his darling wife. And when she looked at him and the moonlight shone on his face, she recognized him too. They embraced one another and kissed and lived happily ever after.*

"One day, when the first signs of spring were just appearing." With this sentence, one can clearly see how the new grass, flowers, and herbs emerge from the frozen ground. One really gets a sense of the triumph of life over hibernation and stasis. Thus, one can also imagine that the two lovers are enlivened by the feeling of spring and that a transition to a more intense way of life is on the horizon.

Just by chance, the two of them encounter one another again. Perhaps it is chance, but then again, perhaps not. They may have taken it to be fate, a happy turn in events that they found one another. They no longer have to feel so lonely and can take some comfort from fellow human company. However, they do not recognize one another as yet. Unlike before when they were reunited at the pond and virtually threw themselves at one another, this time they come together much more slowly and without feeling much desire for one another. Each takes some comfort from the absence they sense in the other.

Both of them have been involved in "shepherding." This could be taken to mean that even though a couple have gone through a period of great alienation, they both still have been involved in doing their everyday chores, such as caring for their children. They are glad that even if passion is missing from their relationship, at least they have restored a loving closeness while they go about the business of everyday life. They feel relieved, despite the fact that passion may never return to the relationship. Mutually getting along with everyday life is also a part of a loving relationship, and where this is absent, a passionate relationship has no real foundation.

In our fairy story, this form of the relationship is just a transitional phase. When the full moon appears again and a certain period of time has elapsed, the shepherd plays a beautiful, sad tune on his flute. This reminds the shepherdess of the time when by the light of the full moon she played a melody sitting at the edge of the pond. She remembers how she saw the body of her beloved emerge from the water.

Now he really sees her and recognizes that she is his beloved wife—and she looks at him and, when the moon shines on his face, also recognizes him. By the light of the moon and under the sign of the moon, they know one another. To be sure, "knowing" one another means here that they also know one another in the biblical sense.[52] A full and complete kind of love is now possible.

The shepherd also plays his flute by the light of the full moon. He too lets himself be influenced by the phase of the full moon. And she recognizes him when the light of the moon shines on his face. The moon-related, emotion-filled moment, which is so strongly influenced by cyclical transformation, allows the two of them to recognize one another in a completely new way. It is no longer a matter of what each of them represents in the world or what external attributes each has. They recognize one another on the basis of a deep, spiritual encounter.

The husband's flute came from the old woman. Apparently it has passed from the hands of the wife and the nixie into his possession. Instead of owning a weapon, he now has a flute. This is clearly what he has been lacking: the capacity to express a whole plethora of feelings, including the abyssal, and a capacity to play with the air. At the beginning of the story, it seemed as though the nixie was demanding all of the objects for herself—at least this is what she did with the flute. However, the flute was clearly intended for the husband. Now, he too has demonstrated that he is capable of playing his own primal song, that he can express the entire complement of feelings, and that his song is at the same time a spiritual song. He can now convey his innermost longings in a very expressive way. And the expression of these feelings also speaks to her deepest feelings. The nuance of feelings which she demonstrated back at the pond is something that he has also become capable of in the meantime. Now they can truly approach one another as partners in a fulfilling love relationship.

They really look at one another—and they recognize one another. Looking at someone and really taking them for who they are—feeling that one is also seen—this is one thing. Recognition, however, goes much further. It means nothing other than loving. The two of them recall their old love, and in this process of recollection, their love blossoms all over again.

At this point, they truly recognize one another. They are no longer torn apart by physical desire, since they have incorporated into themselves the more subtle emotional characteristic of intimacy. As a result, both the nixie and the wise old woman can coexist.

What We Can Learn

In a very subtle way, the fairy story illustrates a laborious developmental process. By the end of which, two people really have been "initiated into love."[53] They have been overwhelmed by passionate emotions—he by eroticism and sexuality, she by grief—and step by step, they have learned to deal with passionate, unbounded feelings. They have directly encountered their emotional selves and, thereby, become more centered. At the same time, they have become capable of participating in a fulfilling love relationship, without feeling the need to suppress any aspect of their emotional lives.

The fairy story teaches us that if we want to live with greater intensity, then we can only do so if we learn to cultivate the quieter feelings. We have to be capable of staying centered even when we feel grief and longing. Yet, how great is the temptation in times of trial to look for external distractions, to constantly seek out people with whom we can share our feelings. In a subtle way, the fairy tale makes it clear that there are times when it is appropriate to speak about our problems, but we have to consciously pick the time and place. Then again, there is also a time when it is appropriate to be silent and to make an effort to stay centered.

The problems which the miller ought to have dealt with at the beginning of the fairy story have now been solved. Under the sign of the moon, the law of life–death–life has been accepted. The notion of life as exclusively beneficent has been forgone. As a result, the tendency toward depression has been alleviated.[54] The nixie can coexist, and the integration of passionate, longing, untrammelled feelings is something that both of the people have managed to accomplish. The nixie is no longer simply a source of terror, and the fear of attraction has clearly diminished.

Dealing with Our Partner's Attraction

However, the greatest thing we can learn from this fairy tale is how to deal with a partner who is in the grips of a powerful attraction to someone else. Attractions like this seem to appear out of the blue, and they cause a great deal of turmoil in a couple's relationship. We are not always prepared to undergo the developmental process that the fairy story recommends. Generally, we are all too eager to issue an ultimatum: either it is him/her or me. If, however, what is at stake is an attraction that does not involve another person, then we are usually prepared to be very generous: we relinquish the partner to whatever is preoccupying them, without putting up much of a fight. As a result, the relationship is only impoverished. The scene of the woman grieving by the edge of the pond does not take place. The hunter is at the bottom of the pond, and the wife goes on with her life in her comfortable little house. And she waits. Perhaps.

In other words, the survival of the relationship depends on whether the scene at the edge of the pond takes place or not. It depends on whether or not there is the experience of loss and whether this loss is then grieved over or not. The likelihood of the partner being won back is also contingent upon whether the other person stays attached to their partner. They have to remember that being attracted to someone else is not just an aspect of character, it is a matter of fate. It is also worth bearing in mind that the problem of attractions occurs quite frequently, and that defending oneself against attraction is not necessarily the answer. It may just result in feelings of depression. Nor can attractions simply be sacrificed. They demand a laborious process of emotional differentiation.

In terms of dealing with the attraction, this fairy tale sets up a particularly appropriate psychic situation: both of them suffer from a nixie complex. Seducing the husband away from the source of his attraction can occur because the wife is able to cultivate new aspects of herself which the husband in turn finds appealing. This is often the case, but it is not invariably so. Of course, it would be fatal if all women were to start trying to find out what attracts men, without paying any attention to their own needs and identities. It just does not work this way, nor does it work in the reverse direction: women and men can only cultivate what is believable and sustainable over the long term, what is fitting in terms of their own personalities and their own levels of development.

When the problem is a collective one and attraction is repressed because it is in vogue to do so, then whatever has been repressed will reemerge in the collective consciousness. The extent to which one can deal with the problem depends on the extent to which this collective problem also corresponds to one's own individual circumstances. If it is "only" a collective problem, then such an existential manifestation of the problem will not ensue the way it does in our fairy tale. Aside from this, confronting the problem of a partner's attraction does not always work out in reality as well as it does here: the fairy tale calls for us to stick by our partner, to express and put up with our feelings, and to work patiently and persistently at changing things. But above all, we are called upon to stay emotionally open to both our partner and to the relationship, whether this be in the context of grief, despair, or longing. If we can employ this kind of life-wisdom when it comes to dealing with attraction, then the wise old woman will help us out—and the nixie will not be far off either!

Notes

1. "The Mermaid in the Pond," in *KHM* 2:181, Manesse, Zurich 1946, 456.

2. Cf. Graumantel, from: *German Folk Tales: New Series*, ed. Elfriede Moser-Rath.

3. Verena Kast, *Joy, Inspiration, Hope*, 157 ff.

4. Verena Kast, *Imagination as Space of Freedom*.

5. Johannes Bolte and Gary Polivka, *Notes on the Grimm Brothers' Children's Fairy Stories and Folk Tales*.

6. Verena Kast, *Father–Daughter, Mother–Son: Freeing Ourselves from the Complexes That Bind Us*, 51 ff., 89ff., 322ff.

7. H. Bächtold-Stäubli, *Dictionary of German Superstition*, vol. 9, 127ff.

8. Ibid., 150.

9. Walter Burkert, *Homo Necans*, 191.

10. Michael Grant and John Hazel, *Dictionary of Classical Myths and Figures*.

11. Marija Gimbutas, *The Language of the Goddess*.

12. Ibid., 111.

13. Ibid.

14. Bächtold-Stäubli, *Dictionary of German Superstition*, vol. 7, 1564.
15. Ibid., 1563.
16. Ibid., vol. 1, 1679.
17. Gimbutas, *Language of the Goddess*, 109.
18. Cf. Kurt Ranke, *Encyclopedia of Fairy Tales*, vol. 2, 707.
19. Kast, *Father–Daughter, Mother–Son*, 109ff.
20. Kast, *Joy, Inspiration, Hope*, 157ff.
21. Verena Kast, *The Dynamics of Symbols: Fundamentals of Jungian Psychology*, 44ff.
22. Kast, *Father–Daughter, Mother–Son*, 109ff.
23. Gimbutas, *Language of the Goddess*, 111.
24. Kast, *Dynamics of Symbols*, 44ff.
25. Verena Kast, "The Little Cow," in *Family Conflicts in Fairy Tales: A Psychological Interpretation*.
26. Gimbutas, *Language of the Goddess*, 113.
27. Burkert, *Homo Necans*, 24.
28. Ibid., 24.
29. Ibid., 72.
30. Ibid., 29.
31. Ibid., 63.
32. Verena Kast, *Grieving: Phases and Opportunities in the Psychological Process*, 158.
33. Verena Kast, *Dealing with Your Feelings and Letting Go*.
34. Verena Kast, *The Creative Leap: Psychological Transformation through Crisis*, 53f.
35. Ingrid Riedel, *The Wise Woman in the Context of Ancient and Contemporary Experiences* [and particularly in this story], 76ff.
36. Riedel, *Wise Woman*, 152ff.; Kast, *Imagination as Space of Freedom*, 109–17.
37. Kast, *Imagination as Space of Freedom*, 109ff.

38. Verena Kast, *The Devil with the Three Golden Hairs: On Trusting One's Own Fate*.

39. P. Zaunert, *German Fairy Tales since Grimm*, 145 (Unfortunately, the 1964 edition did not include the story).

40. Verena Kast, *How to Achieve Autonomy: Fairy Tales From a Psychological Perspective*, 15ff.

41. Reidel, *Wise Woman*, 18ff.

42. Marie-Louise von Franz, "With the Black Woman. The Interpretation of a Fairy Tale," in *Fairy Tale Research and Depth Psychology*, 95ff.

43. Kast, *Imagination as Space of Freedom*, 109–17.

44. Kast, *Creative Leap*, 2.

45. Kast, *Dynamics of Symbols*, 181.

46. Kast, *Folktales as Therapy*.

47. Bächthold-Stäubli, *Dictionary of German Superstition*, vol. 9, 152.

48. Verena Kast, *Love in the Fairy Tale*.

49. Gimbutas, *Language of the Goddess*, 67.

50. Ibid., 256.

51. Kast, *Dealing with Your Feelings*, 27ff.

52. Genesis 4:1.

53. Riedel, *Wise Woman*, 76ff.

54. Kast, *Father–Daughter, Mother–Son*, 97ff.

Bibliography

Bächtold-Stäubli, H., ed. *Dictionary of German Superstition*. Berlin, Leipzig 1936–37.

Bolte, Johannes and Gary Polivka. *Notes on the Grimm Brothers' Children's Fairy Stories and Folk Tales*. Hildesheim 1963.

Burkert, Walter. *Homo Necans*. Berlin, New York 1972.

Franz, Marie-Louise von. "With the Black Woman: The Interpretation of a Fairy Tale." *Fairy Tale Research and Depth Psychology*, Wilhelm Laiblin, ed. Darmstadt.

Gimbutas, Marija. *The Language of the Goddess*. San Francisco 1989.

Grant, Michael and John Hazel. *Dictionary of Classical Myths and Figures*. Munich 1980.

Kast, Verena. "Animus and Anima: Spiritual Growth and Separation from the Parental Complexes." *Harvest* vol. 39, 1993

————. "A Concept of Participation." *The Interactive Field in Analysis*. Wilmette: Chiron, 1996.

————. *The Creative Leap: Psychological Transformation through Crisis*. Wilmette: Chiron, 1990.

————. *Dealing with Your Feelings and Letting Go*. Newreiburg 1994.

————. *The Devil with the Three Golden Hairs: On Trusting One's Own Fate*. Stuttgart 1984, 91(6).

————. *The Dynamics of Symbols: Fundamentals of Jungian Psychology*. New York: Fromm International, 1992.

————. *Escaping Fear and Symbiosis*. Olten 1982, 91(9), dtv 15031, 91(5).

————. *Fairy Tales for the Psyche*. New York: Continuum, 1996.

————. *Family Conflicts in the Fairy Tale: A Psychological Interpretation*. Olten 1984, 94(4), dtv 15042.

————. *Father–Daughter, Mother–Son: Freeing Ourselves from the Complexes That Bind Us*. Rockport, Mass.: Element Shaftesbury, Dorset.

————. *Folktales as Therapy*. New York: Fromm International, 1995.

————. *Grieving: Phases and Opportunities in the Psychological Process*. Stuttgart, 1982, 92 (13).

————. *Growth through Emotions: Interpretation of Fairy Tales*. New York: Fromm International, 1993.

————. *How to Achieve Autonomy: Fairy Tales From a Psychological Perspective*. Olten 1986, 89(7).

————. *Imagination as Space of Freedom*. New York: Fromm International, 1993.

————. *Joy, Inspiration, Hope*. Austin: Texas University Press, 1991; New York: Fromm International, 1994.

————. *Letting Go and Finding Yourself: Separating from Your Children*. New York: Continuum, 1994.

————. "The Little Cow." *Family Conflicts in Fairy Tales: A Psychological Interpretation*. Olten 1984, 94(4), dtv 15042.

————. *Love in the Fairy Tale*. Olten 1992.

————. *The Nature of Loving: Patterns of Human Relationship*. Wilmette: Chiron, 1986.

————. *Sisyphus: A Jungian Approach to Midlife Crises*. Daimon, Einsiedeln 1991.

————. *A Time to Mourn: Growing through the Grief Process*. Daimon, Einsiedeln 1988.

————. "The Water Sprite in the Pond." *Escaping Fear and Symbiosis*. Olten 1982, 91(9), dtv 15031, 91(5).

Mario, Jacoby; Verena Kast; and Ingrid Riedel. *Witches, Ogres, and the Devil's Daughter*. Boston and London: Shambhala, 1992.

Moser-Rath, Elfriede, ed. *German Folk Tales: New Series*. Düsseldorf, Cologne 1966.

Ranke, Kurt, ed. *Encyclopedia of Fairy Tales*, vol. 2. Berlin 1979.

Riedel, Ingrid. *The Wise Woman in the Context of Ancient and Contemporary Experiences*. Olten 1989.

Zaunert, P. *German Fairy Tales since Grimm*. Jena 1922. [In the 1964 edition, the fairy story "The Mermaid in the Pond" has unfortunately not been included.]